Civil War Maps

A Graphic Index to the
*Atlas to Accompany the Official Records
of the Union and Confederate Armies*

*The Hermon Dunlap Smith Center for the History of Cartography
Occasional Publication No. 1*

REFERENCE USE ONLY
NEW HANOVER COUNTY PUBLIC LIBRARY

NORTH CAROLINA ROOM
NEW HANOVER COUNTY PUBLIC LIBRARY

*The Hermon Dunlap Smith Center for the History of Cartography
Occasional Publication No. 1*

Civil War Maps

A Graphic Index to the
*Atlas to Accompany the Official Records
of the Union and Confederate Armies*

by
Noel S. O'Reilly,
David C. Bosse,
and Robert W. Karrow, Jr.

NEW HANOVER COUNTY
PUBLIC LIBRARY
201 CHESTNUT STREET
WILMINGTON, N. C. 28401

Chicago
The Newberry Library
1987

Copyright 1987, The Newberry Library

Base maps reproduced under
American Map Company copyright release #18991

ISBN 0-911028-36-6

Typesetting and Printing by
The University of Chicago Printing Department

Available from
The Newberry Library Bookshop
60 W. Walton St.
Chicago, Illinois 60610

Preface

It has long been one of the aims of the Center for the History of Cartography to initiate a series of occasional publications. With this volume we succeed in doing so. Our hope is that we shall be able to bring out one or two similar volumes each year, covering a wide variety of subjects in the history of cartography. While we have four or five manuscripts in reserve at this time, we hope they will soon emerge in print, and urge all interested scholars to submit to us material which seems suitable for inclusion in our new series.

David Buisseret
Director, Hermon Dunlap Smith
Center for the History of Cartography

Contents

Introduction	7
Index Maps	11
Alabama	11
Arkansas	12
Florida	13
Georgia	14
Kansas	21
Kentucky	22
Louisiana	23
Maryland	24
Mississippi	25
Missouri	28
New Mexico	29
North Carolina	30
North Dakota	33
Ohio	34
Pennsylvania	35
South Carolina	36
Tennessee	38
Texas	43
Virginia	44
West Virginia	58
Virginia/Maryland Theater	59
United States	62
Scales of Maps	67

Introduction

Reliance on maps as a tool of military planning resulted in the creation of many thousand cartographic documents during the American Civil War. By the war's end, map production, both in the field and in the respective War Departments, had achieved numbers unprecedented in American military cartography. Federal officers alone were issued 20,938 map sheets in 1864, and 24,591 in 1865.[1] This is in sharp contrast to the state of topographical intelligence facing the opposing armies in 1861. At that time there existed few maps of the interior South suitable for military purposes. Neither government had anticipated the need for large-scale mapping; consequently, several initial campaigns suffered from tactical blunders. Contemporary and post-war accounts lament the dearth of suitable maps, citing specific instances where ignorance of the location of a road or stream influenced the outcome of engagements. Expansion of the Topographical Corps, advances in reproduction technology, and improvements in the dissemination of topographical information eventually alleviated the problem of map supply, particularly among the Federal armies.[2]

Conscious of their historical value and fearing loss or destruction, Congress authorized the retention of textual and cartographic documents relating to the war in the spring of 1864.[3] The Confederate government also maintained official reports and correspondence, many of which were captured when Richmond fell in April, 1865. Unfortunately, numerous Confederate maps were lost at that time, some being intentionally burned while others were put on an archives train never to be seen again.[4] While untold maps failed to survive the war, officers often kept the maps in their possession, thereby helping to preserve the cartographic record.

Reconstruction brought with it public interest in an unbiased account of the conflict based on government documents. This led to the publication of the *War of the Rebellion: A Compilation of the Official Records of the Union and Confederate Armies*. The task of compiling, sorting, and editing this material was such that the first volume did not appear until 1881. Eight years later, the War Department began work on *The Atlas to Accompany the Official Records of the Union and Confederate Armies*.

The atlas contains 1,006 maps and plans, 966 relating to military operations in the field. The latter consist of reconnaissance sketches, battlefield maps of troop positions and movements, and small-scale campaign maps. Few maps actually used in battle, however, are found in the atlas.[5] The majority are redrawings of the maps which accompanied Federal and Confederate reports. Others were found on file in the War Department bureaus or were solicited from commanding officers. An important category of maps in the atlas is battlefield surveys made after the war. A number of these first appeared in *Military Operations of the Armies of the Potomac and James, May 4th, 1864 to April 9th, 1865* (Washington, 1869). This survey, conducted by Nathaniel Michler, John Weyss, Peter Michie, and others, was one of several remapping projects accomplished between 1867 and 1890.[6]

The laborious preparation of the atlas was overseen by Captain Charles Duvall Cowles. Due to the diversity of cartographic material, maps had to be reduced, enlarged, to some extent corrected, and finally engraved. A note indicating sources can be found on each map reproduced. Confederate cartography is represented, but less than twenty-five per cent of the maps are of Southern origin. The atlas is grouped in four parts, being military operations in the field, a general topographical map of the eastern United States on twenty-five plates, military divisions and departments shown on nine base maps of the United States, and a miscellaneous section displaying uniforms, ordnance, ambulance service, flags, and badges.

Maps relating to campaigns are largely arranged by chronology to facilitate use with the *Official Records*. Exceptions to this occur where maps are grouped together on a plate for the best fit or were discovered too late to be included in the proper sequence.[7] For these reasons, and because operations continued simultaneously in the different theatres of the war, the atlas lacks any logical geographical sequence. Occasionally there is some continuity when a number of maps from one campaign are reproduced together or on successive plates. More often, maps from several states share the same plate. Faced with this idiosyncratic arrangement, the user must necessarily rely on an index to locate maps.

The inadequacies of the atlas index have been thoroughly examined by Dallas Irvine in his guide to the *Official Records*.[8] Essentially, there are two flaws which limit the usefulness of the index. Firstly, it often fails to distinguish between a particular campaign or operation and the place or geographic feature from which it takes its name. Secondly, where there is duplication of place names within a state, the index does not provide a subdivided entry to aid in distinguishing one from another. An example from Irvine will illustrate these drawbacks. The entry for New Hope Church, Georgia lists fifteen maps. These actually represent five different localities of the same name, with no indication of the engagements fought at New Hope Church from May 25 to June 5, 1864. Four of the maps are of sufficient scale to be helpful in researching the battle, but one must search the atlas for each map entry in order to discover them.

To provide an alternative to the atlas' cumbersome system of indexing, compilation of a graphic index was begun at the Newberry Library in 1981. The purpose of this index is to graphically portray the sheet lines of each map in the atlas so that geographic coverage is unambiguous. In this way the user can readily determine if an entry in the typographic index for Bull Run is a large-scale plan or a map of northern Virginia. A graphic index has the further advantage of allowing the user to browse through maps of the same area, something not possible with the design of the atlas.

The maps in this index are arranged alphabetically by state, and within each state by the sequential ordering of the maps in the atlas. The number of index maps for a state is dependent on the number of maps in the atlas, so that Virginia, the scene of continual operations from 1861 to 1865, requires more index maps than Arkansas. Using Tennessee as an example, the outline for the map of the Stone's River Campaign (atlas plate no. 31:2*) preceeds the outline for the map of the Knoxville area (atlas plate no. 48:2&). The number to the left of the colon is the plate number (printed in roman numerals in the atlas), the number to the right of the colon is the map number (most atlas plates contain two or more maps). In the examples above, the asterisk (*) following the first number indicates that the map shows at least some landowners' names. The ampersand (&) following the second number indicates a map judged to contain a significant level of topographical detail.

Many plans of battles, fortifications, and cities are drawn at such a large scale that it is impractical to attempt to show their actual outlines in the index. In these cases, a small black square is used to indicate the location of the plan. A "Key to large-scale plans" lists these plans, by county, with their atlas plate numbers.

Finally, an appendix gives the representative fractions of all maps for which scale was determined. If a given atlas plate number does not appear in this list, no scale was given on the map and there was insufficient topographical detail to calculate the scale. It should be remembered that these scales refer to the original edition of the atlas, not to later reprints which may be somewhat reduced.

Copies of the atlas can be found in most libraries. In addition to the original issue, editions were reprinted by the Atlas Publishing Co. (*Atlas of the War of the Rebellion*: New York, 1892–first forty plates only), Thomas Yoseloff (*The Official Atlas of the Civil War*: New York, 1958), and Fairfax Press (*The Official Military Atlas of the Civil War*: New York, 1983). Anyone interested in southern agriculture, transportation networks, demographics, or genealogy should be aware of these maps. Many represent the earliest large-scale mapping of portions of the South. It is hoped that this index will aid users of the atlas in discovering these gems of historical geography in which new and surprising insights await the researcher.

David C. Bosse

NOTES

1. Report of the Chief of Engineers in: *Report of the Secretary of War, 1864.* (Washington: G.P.O., 1865), vol. 2, p. 927; Report of the Chief of Engineers in: *Report of the Secretary of War, 1865,* (Washington: G.P.O., 1866), vol. 2, p. 919.
2. Nettesheim, Daniel D. "Topographical Intelligence and the American Civil War." Masters Thesis, U.S. Army Command and General Staff College, Fort Leavenworth, KS, 1978.
3. Commanger, Henry S. Introduction to *The Official Atlas of the Civil War.* (New York: Thomas Yoseloff, 1958).
4. Campbell, Albert. "The Lost War Maps of the Confederates," *Century Magazine,* vol. 35, no. 3, 1888, pp. 479-481.
5. Aimone, Alan C. *The Official Records of the American Civil War: A Researcher's Guide.* U.S.M.A. Library Bulletin no. 11. (West Point, New York: United States Military Academy, 1972), p. 16.
6. Lilley, David A. "Anticipating the Atlas to Accompany the Official Records," *Lincoln Herald,* vol. 84, no. 1, Spring, 1982, pp. 37-42.
7. Irvine, Dallas. *Military Operations of the Civil War: A Guide-Index to the Official Records of the Union and Confederate Armies, 1861-1865.* 5 vols. (Washington: National Archives and Records Service, 1968-80), vol. 1, p. 30.
8. *Ibid.,* pp. 31-33.

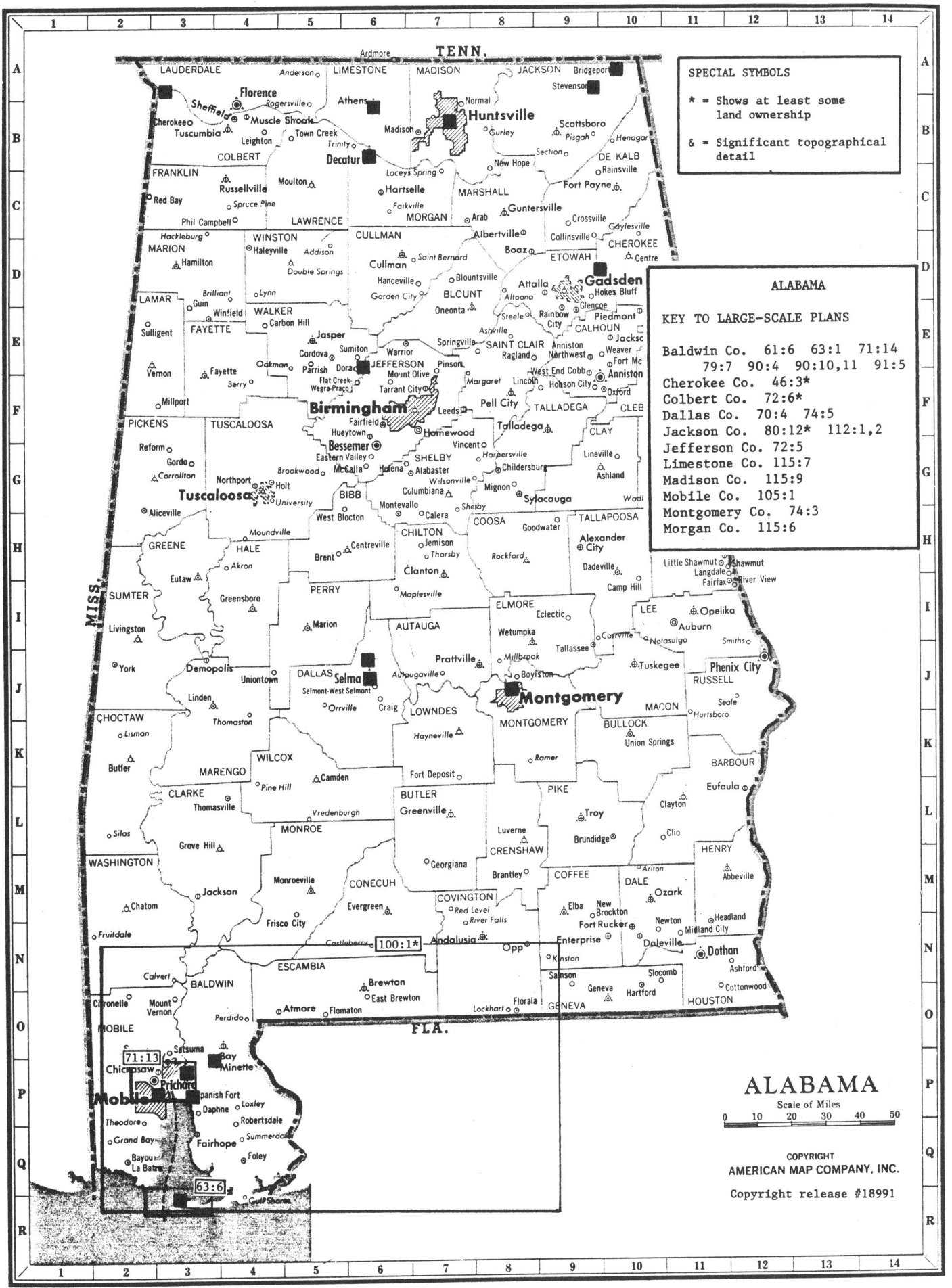

ARKANSAS

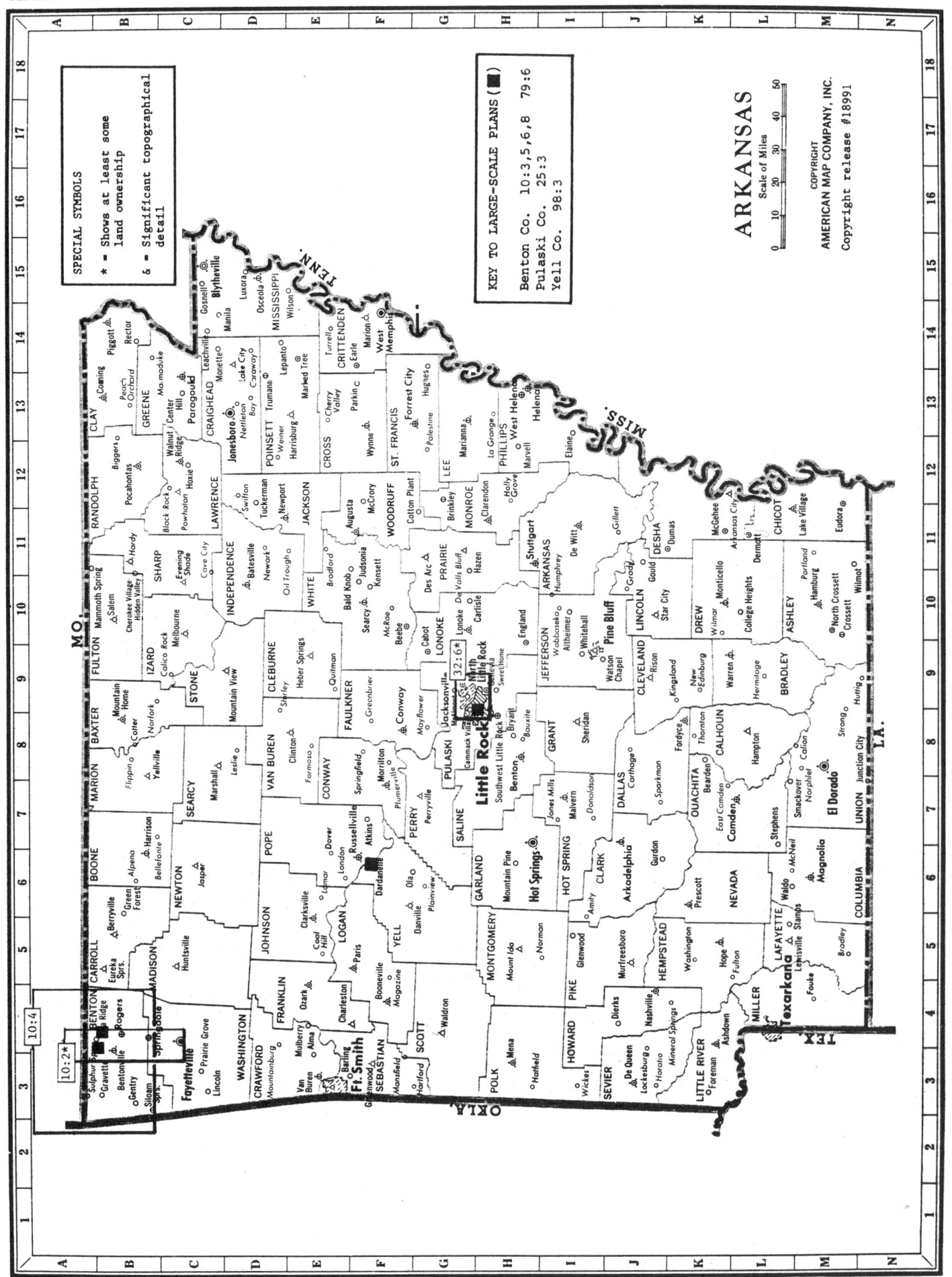

FLORIDA

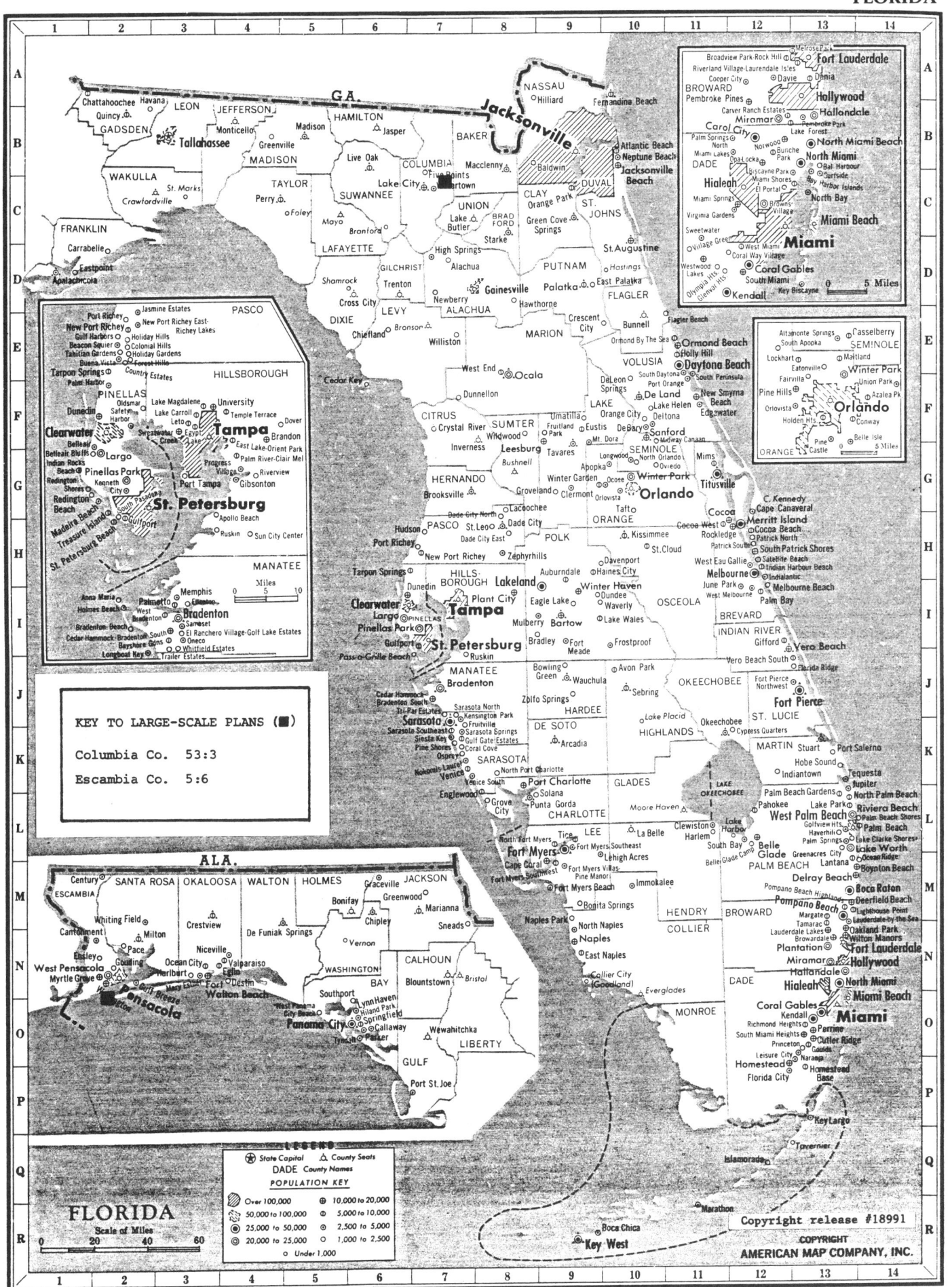

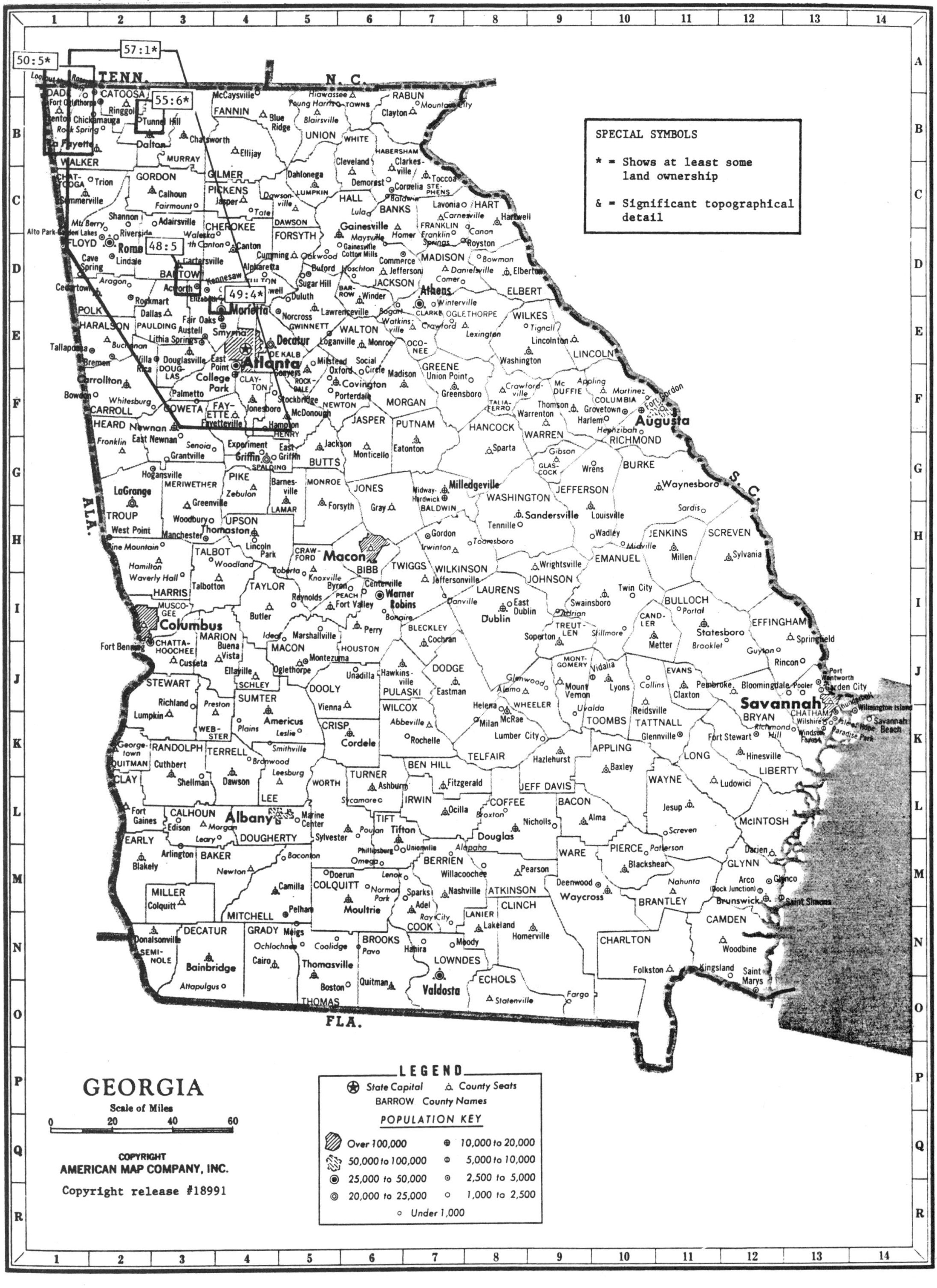

GEORGIA (1 of 7)

SPECIAL SYMBOLS

* = Shows at least some land ownership

& = Significant topographical detail

GEORGIA

Scale of Miles: 0 – 20 – 40 – 60

COPYRIGHT
AMERICAN MAP COMPANY, INC.
Copyright release #18991

LEGEND

- ⊛ State Capital
- △ County Seats
- BARROW County Names

POPULATION KEY

- Over 100,000
- 50,000 to 100,000
- 25,000 to 50,000
- 20,000 to 25,000
- 10,000 to 20,000
- 5,000 to 10,000
- 2,500 to 5,000
- 1,000 to 2,500
- Under 1,000

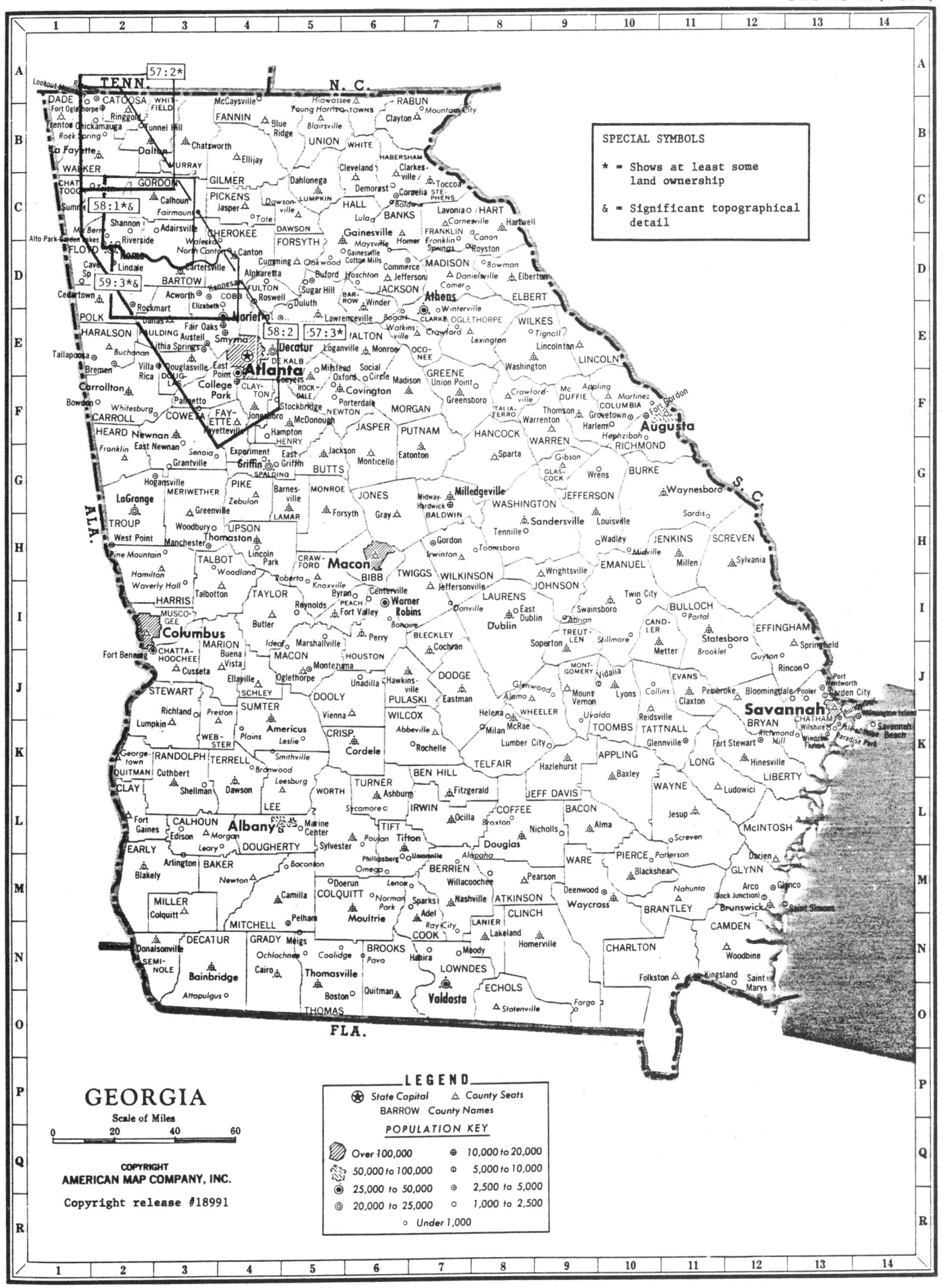

GEORGIA (3 of 7)

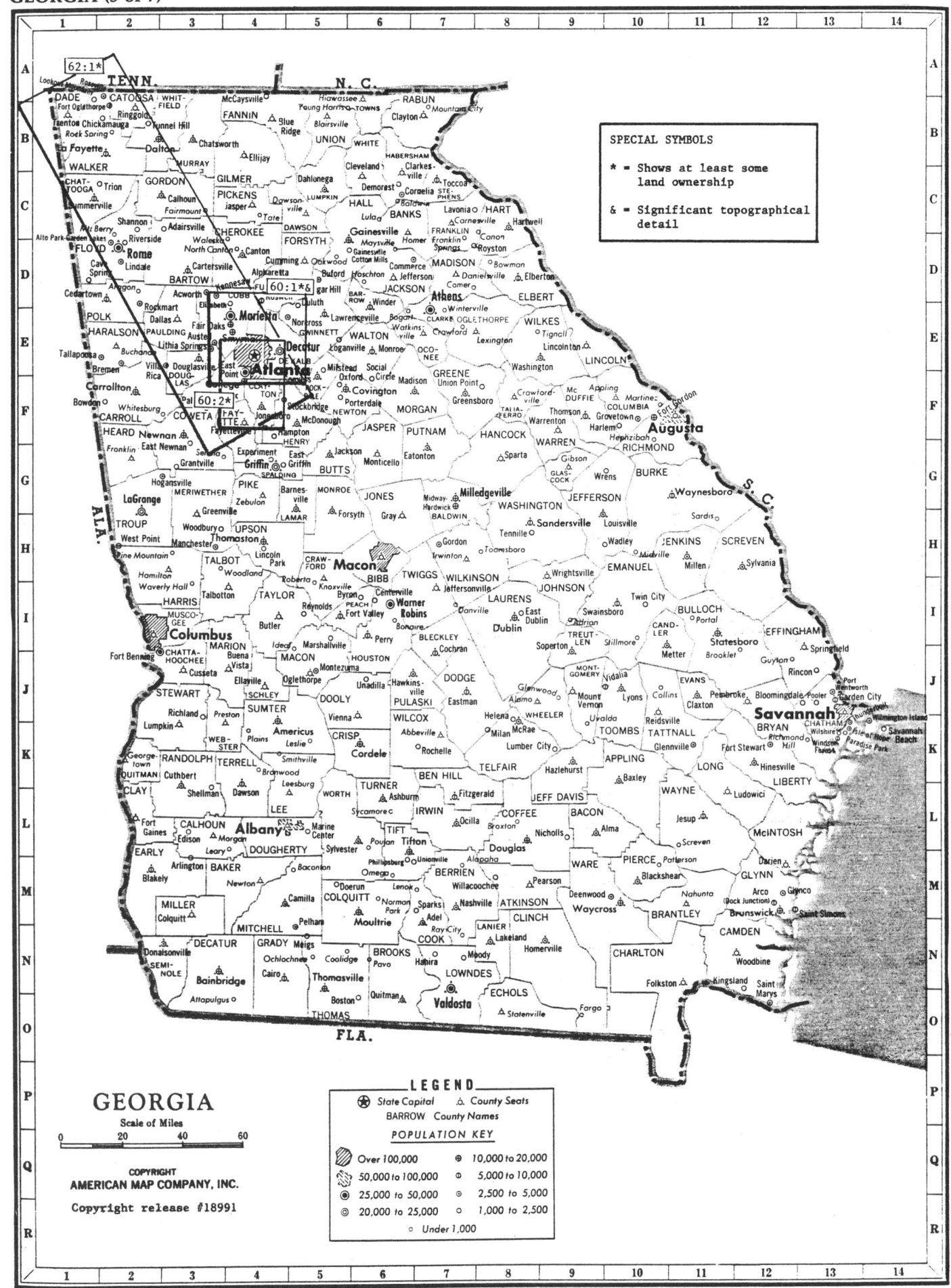

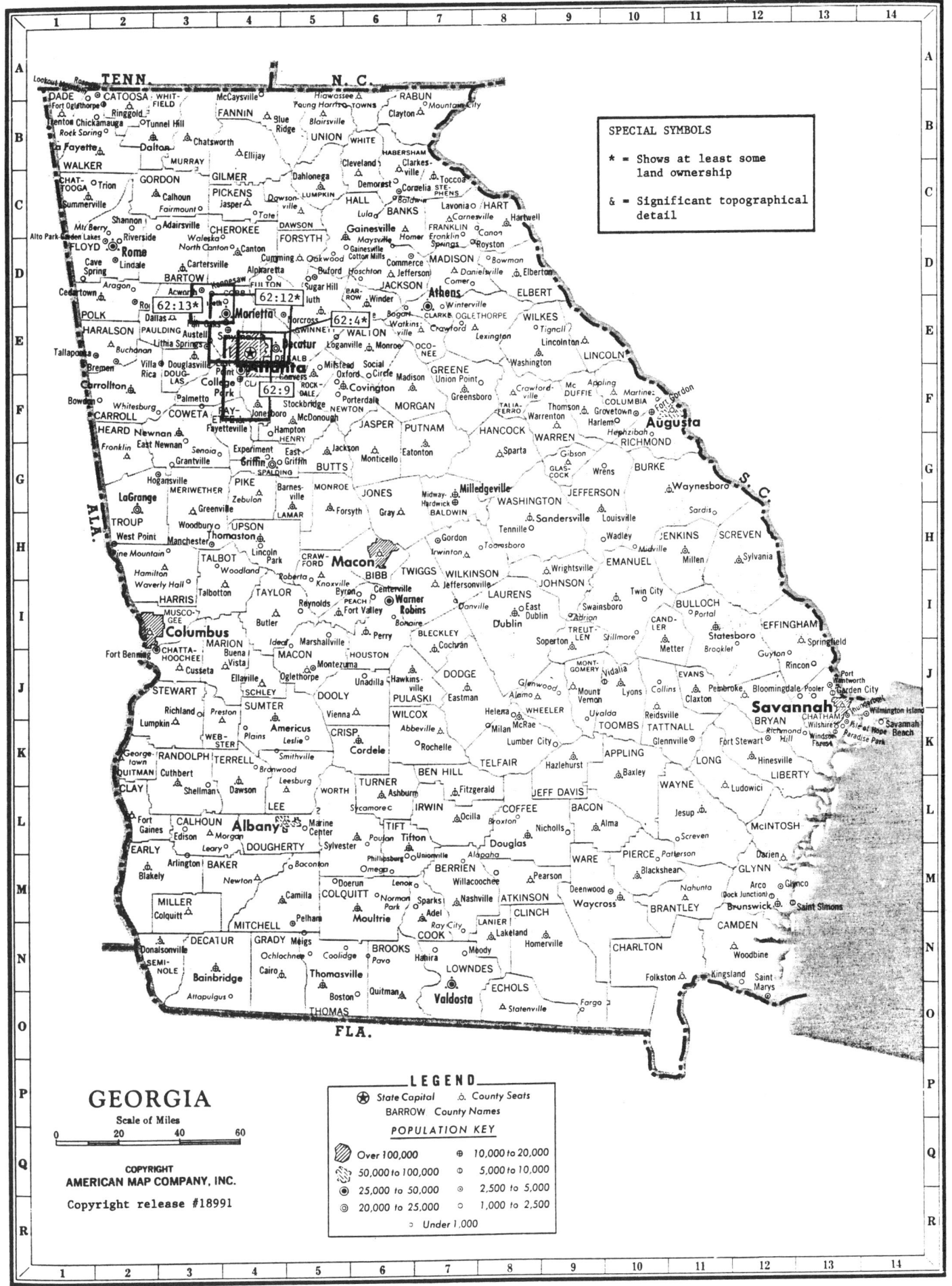

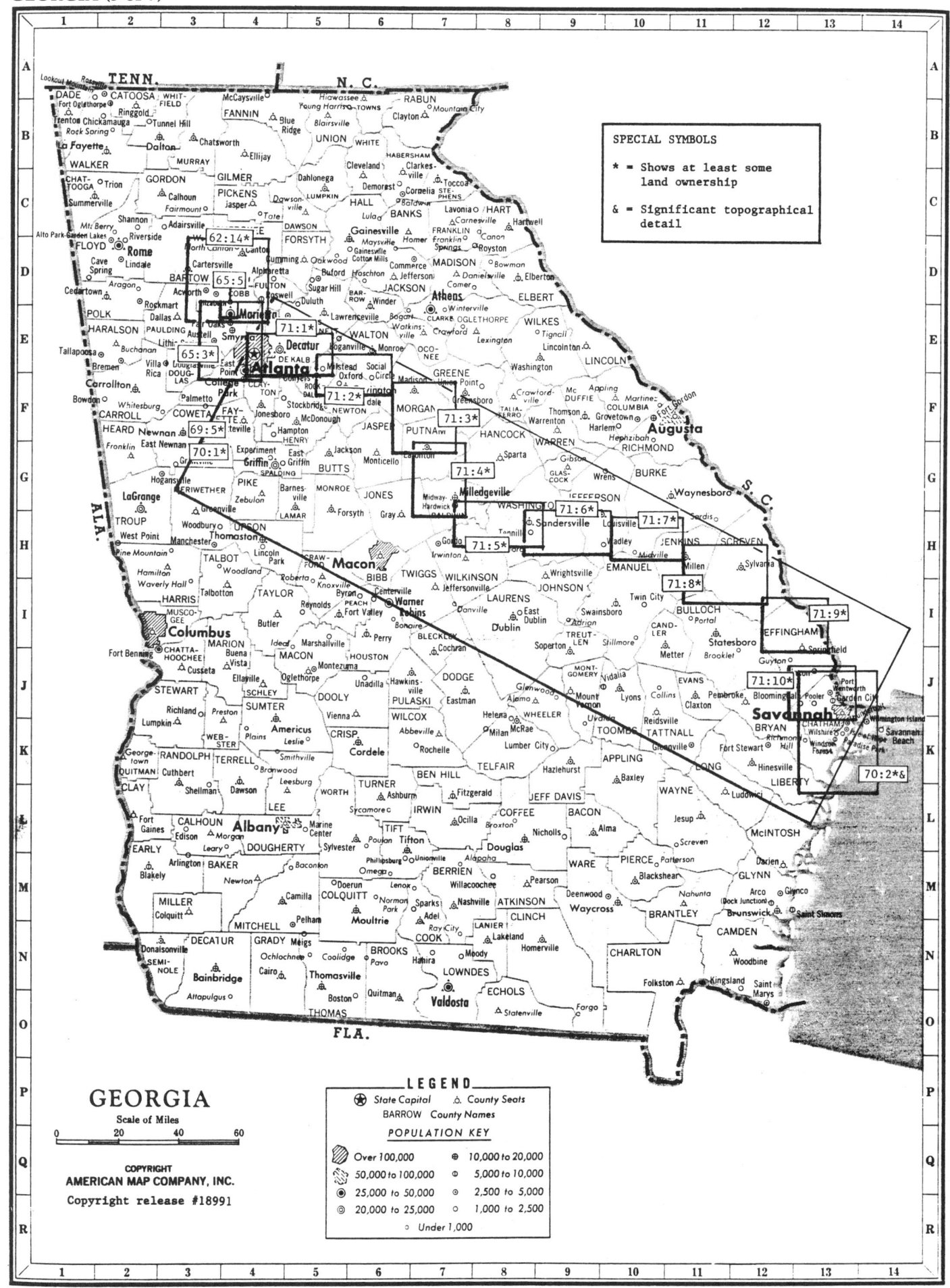

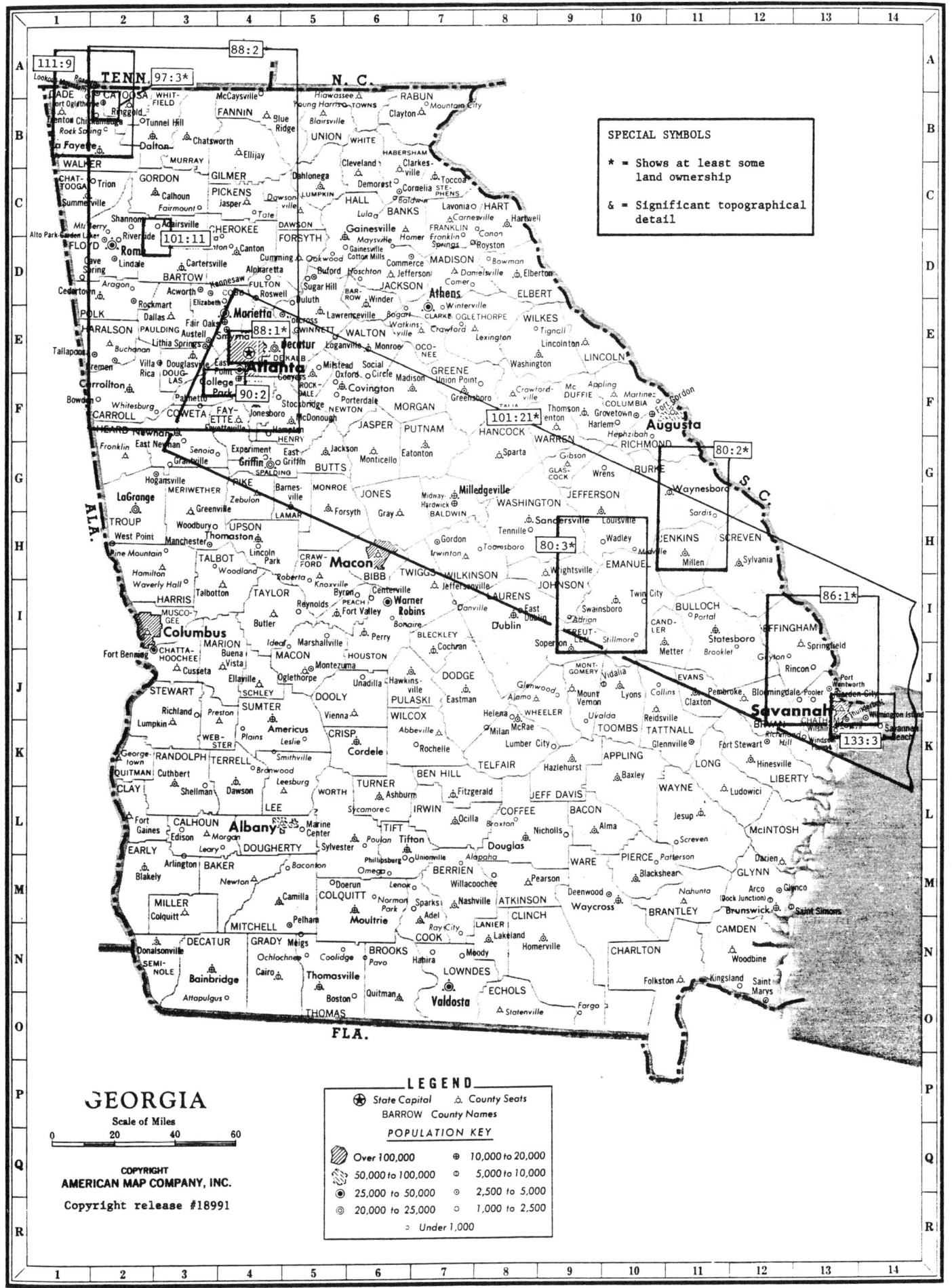

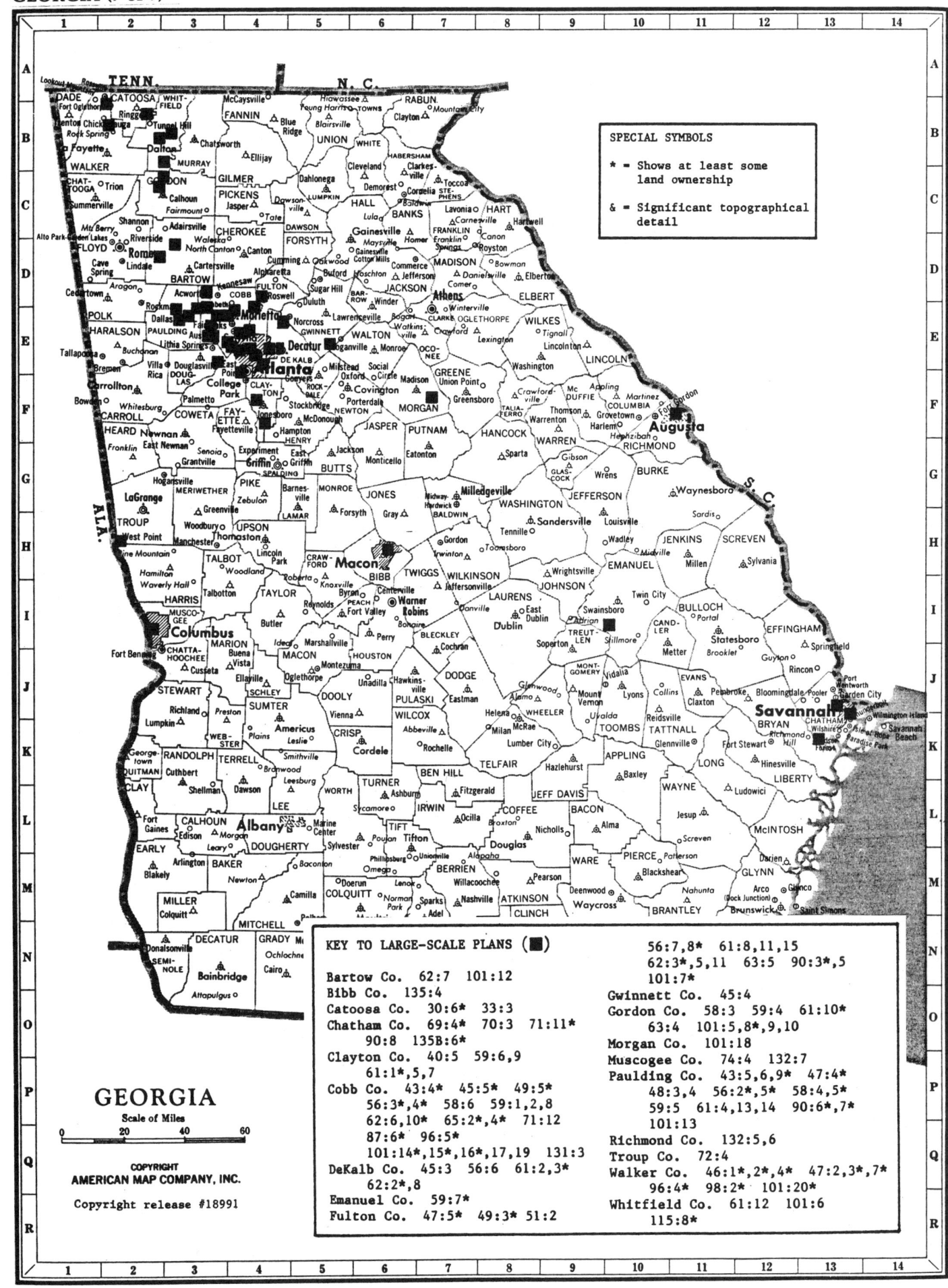

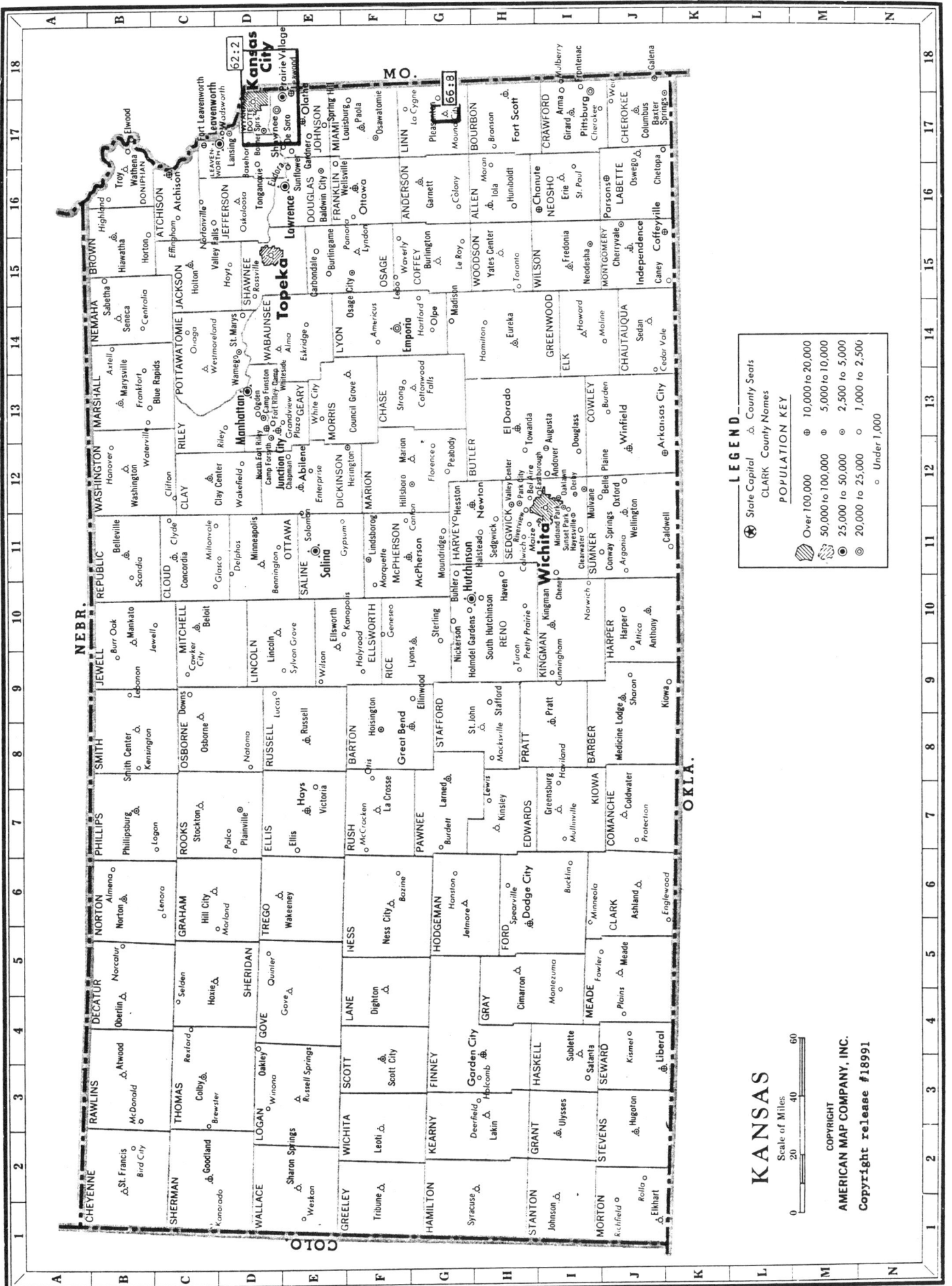

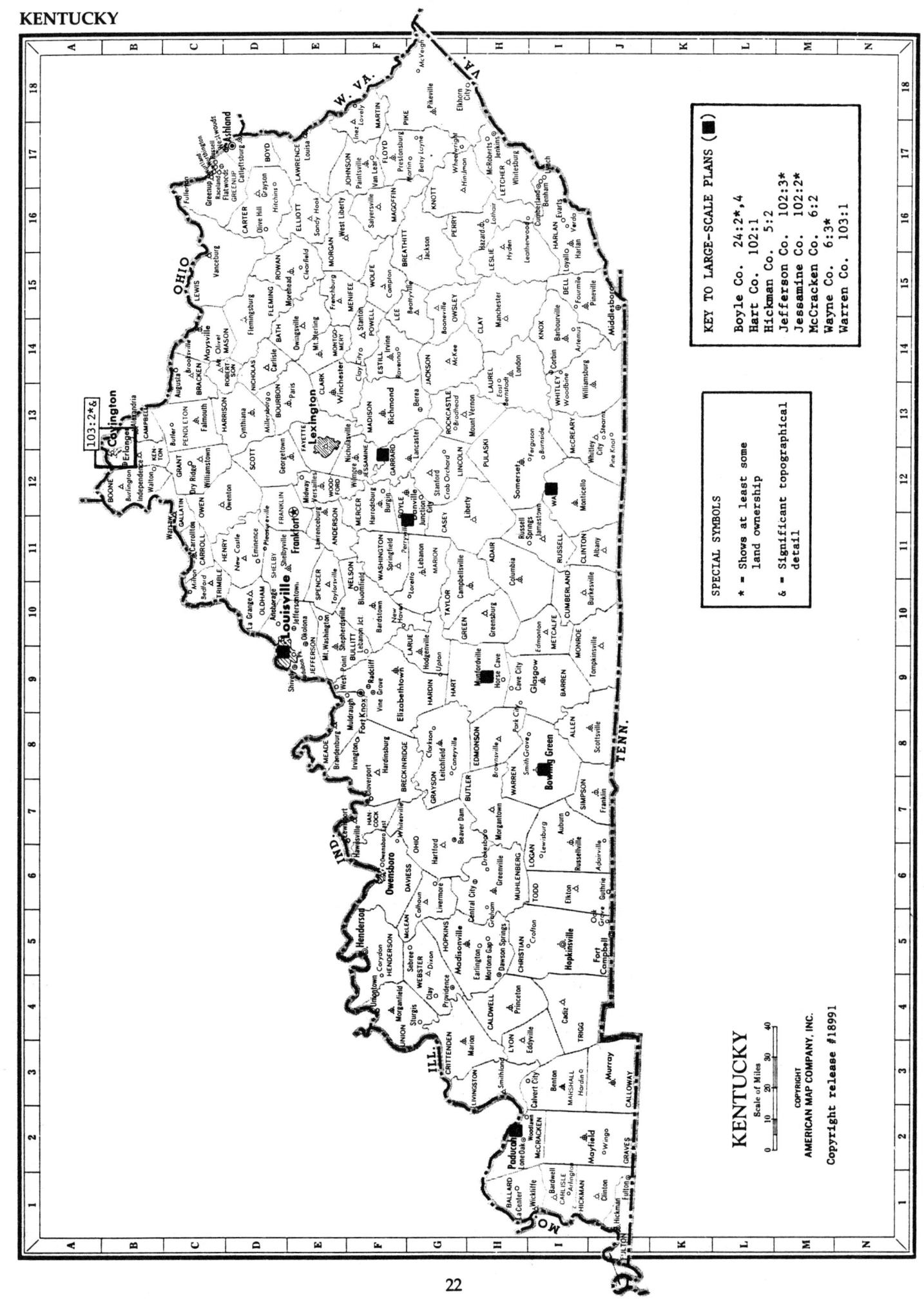

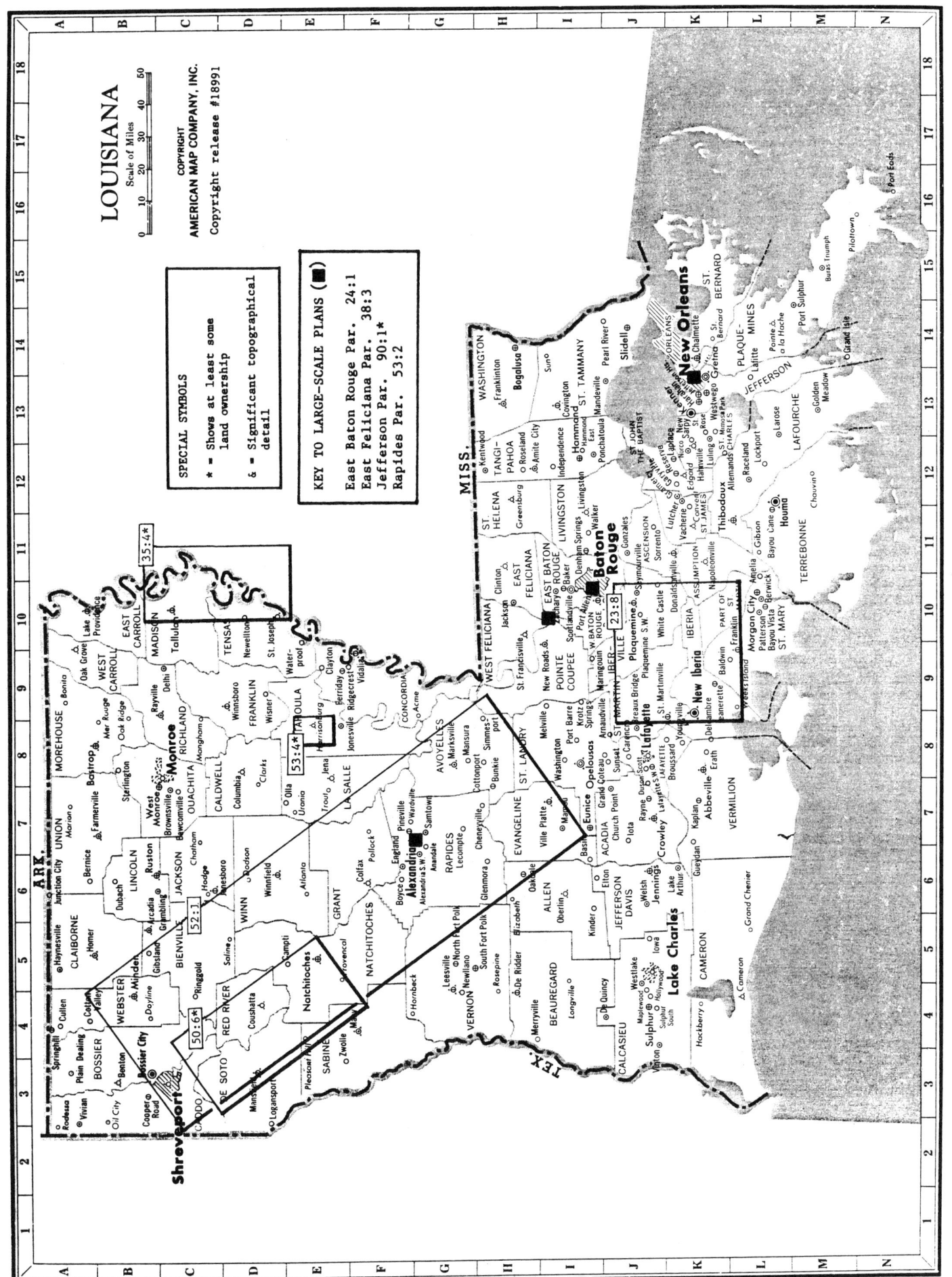

MARYLAND

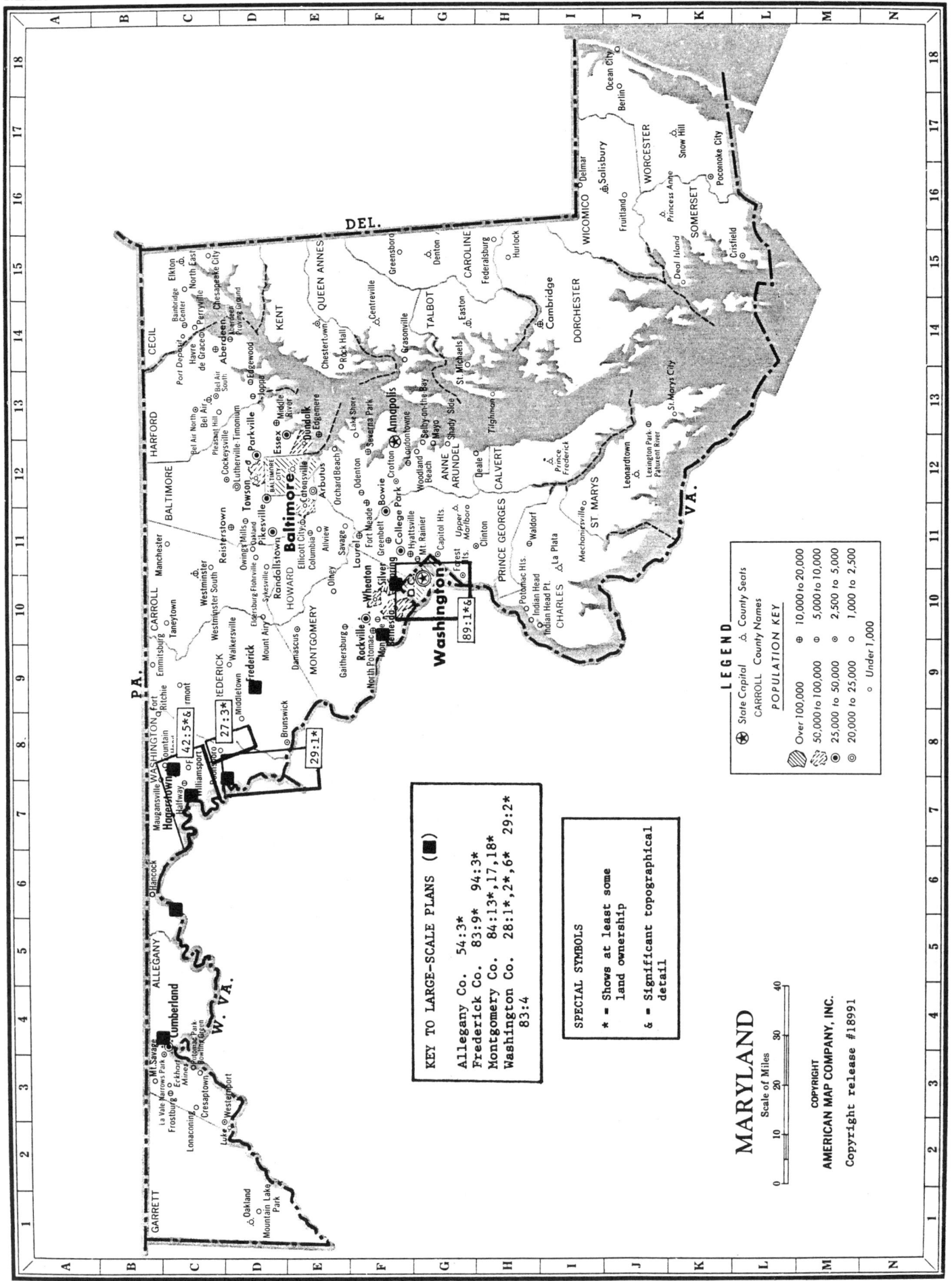

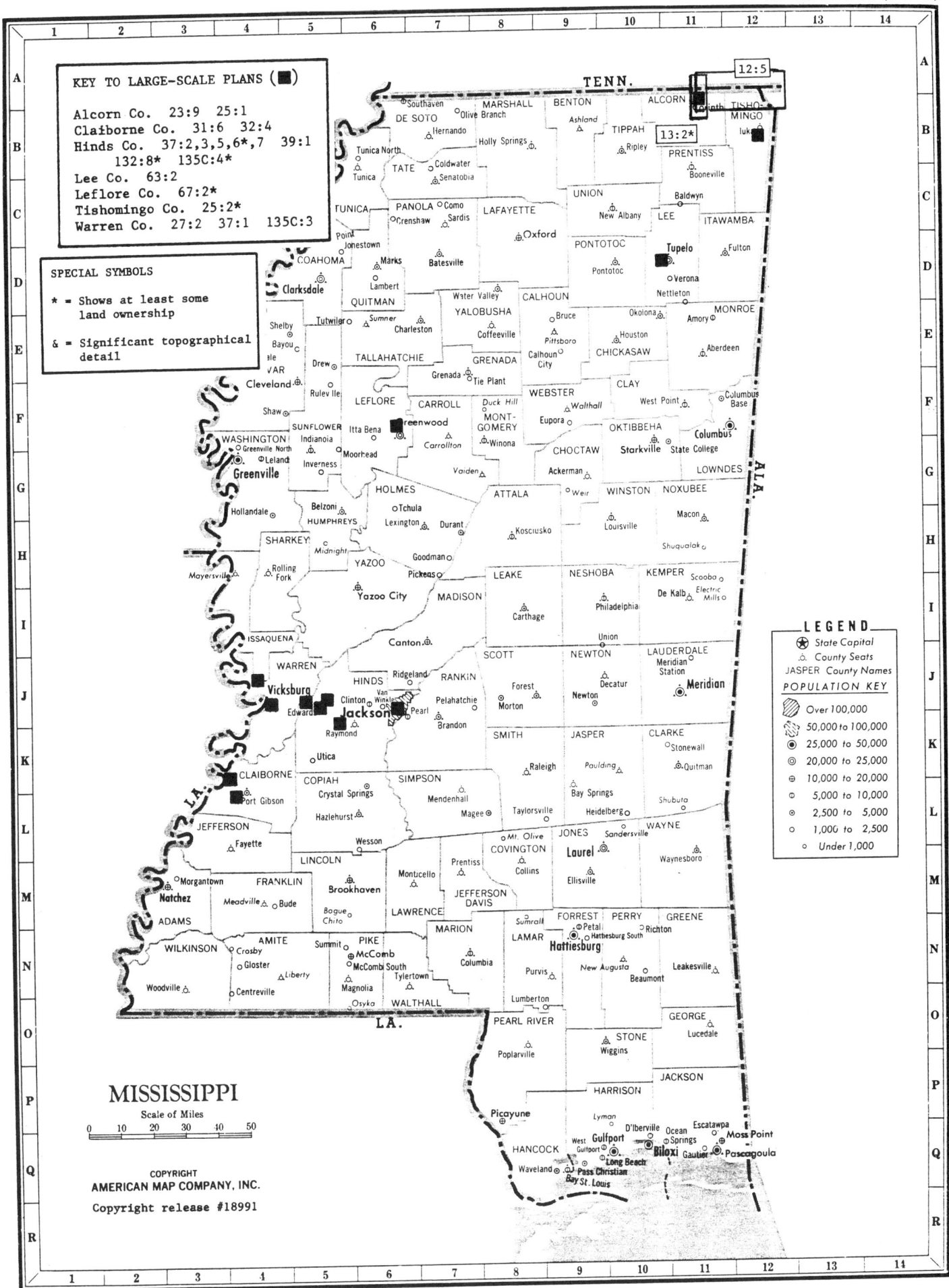

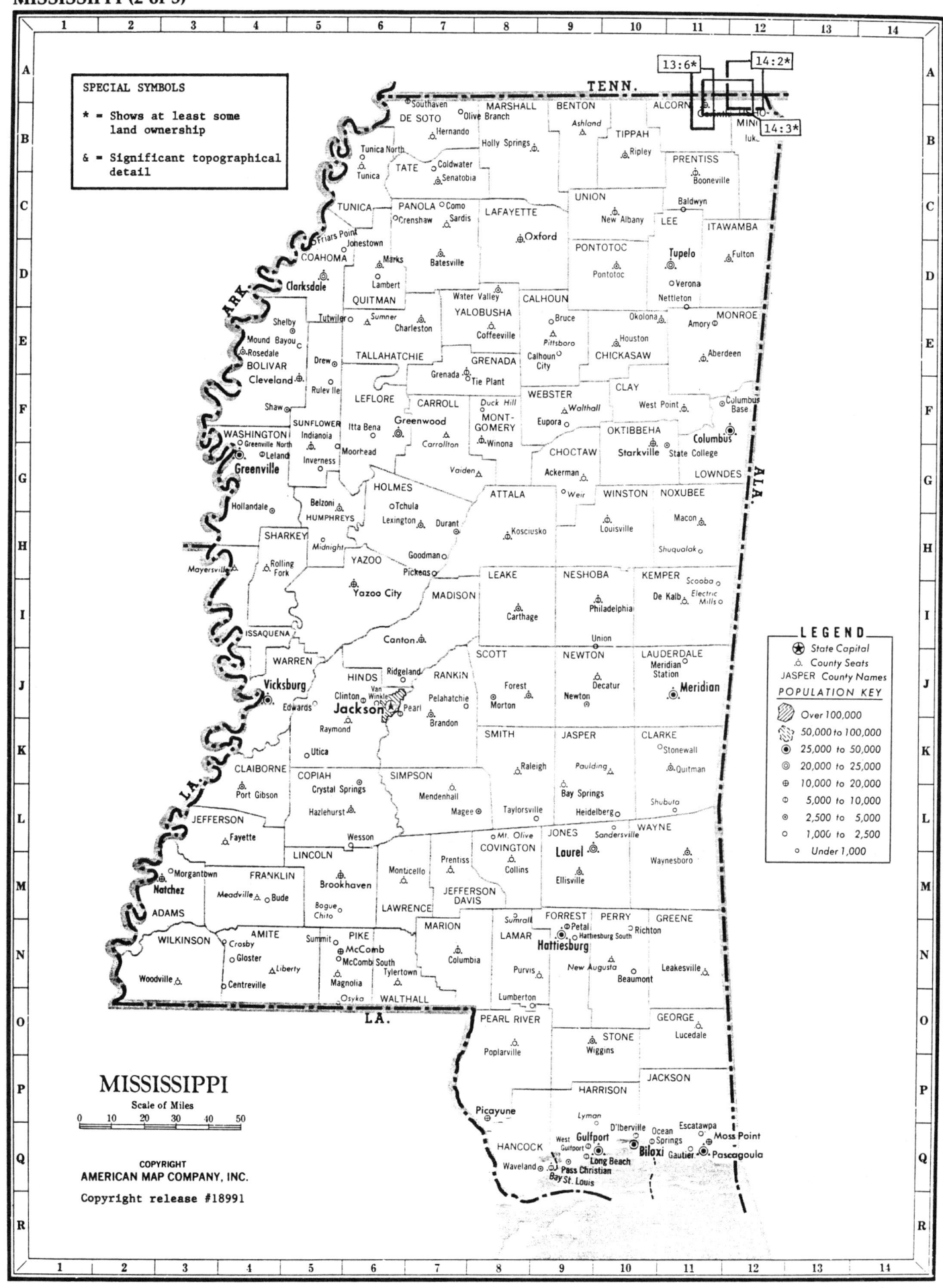

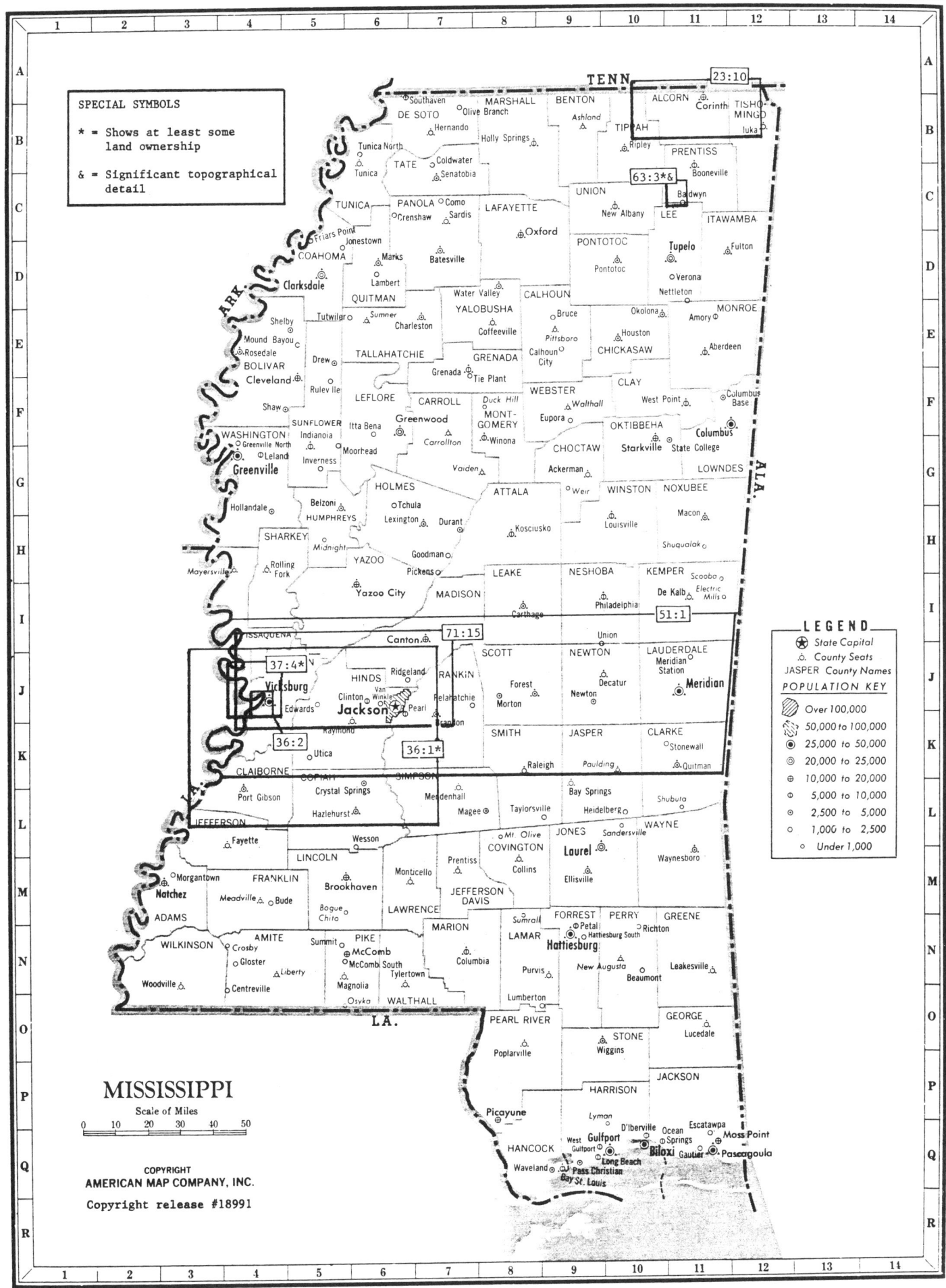

MISSOURI

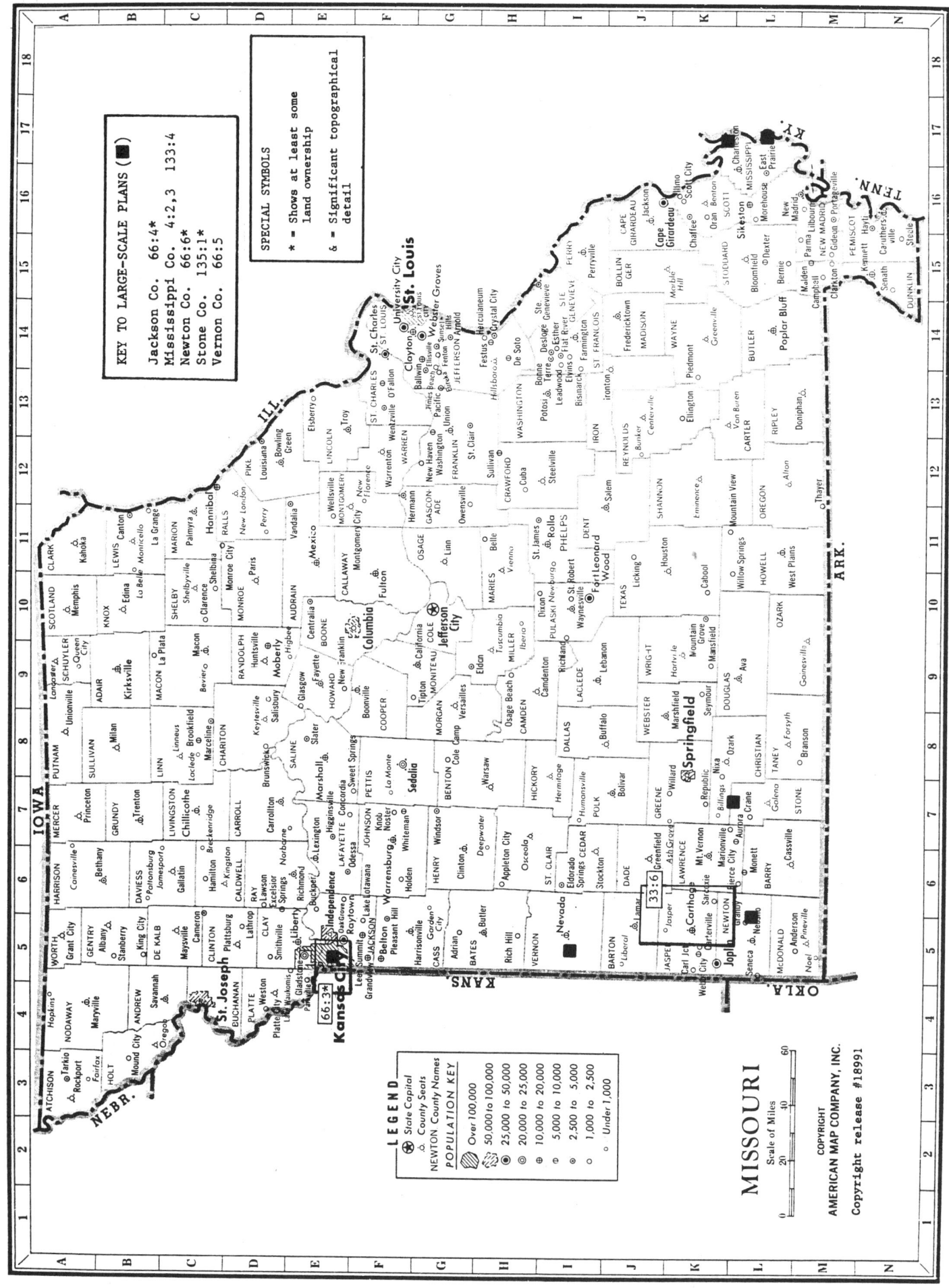

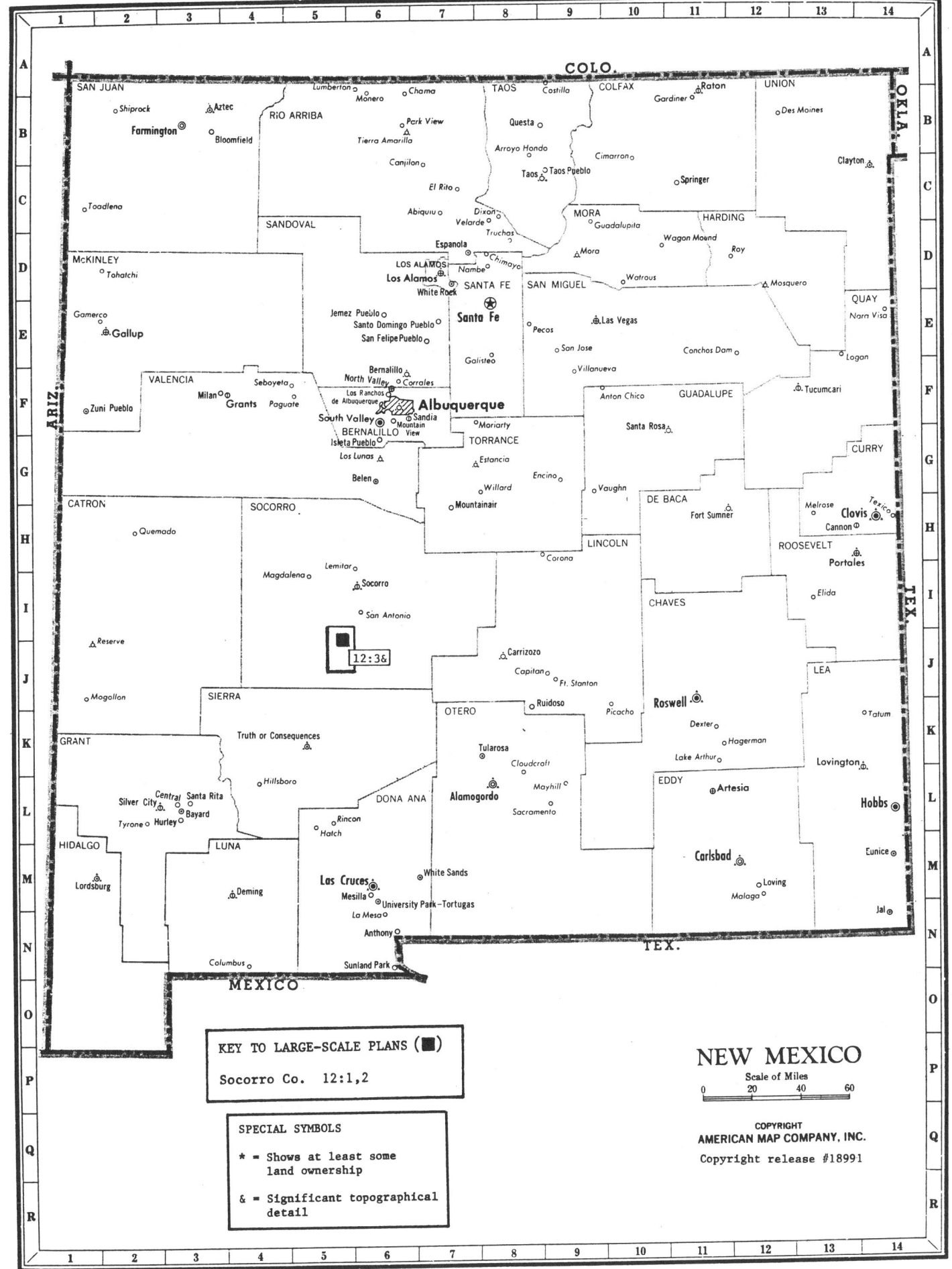

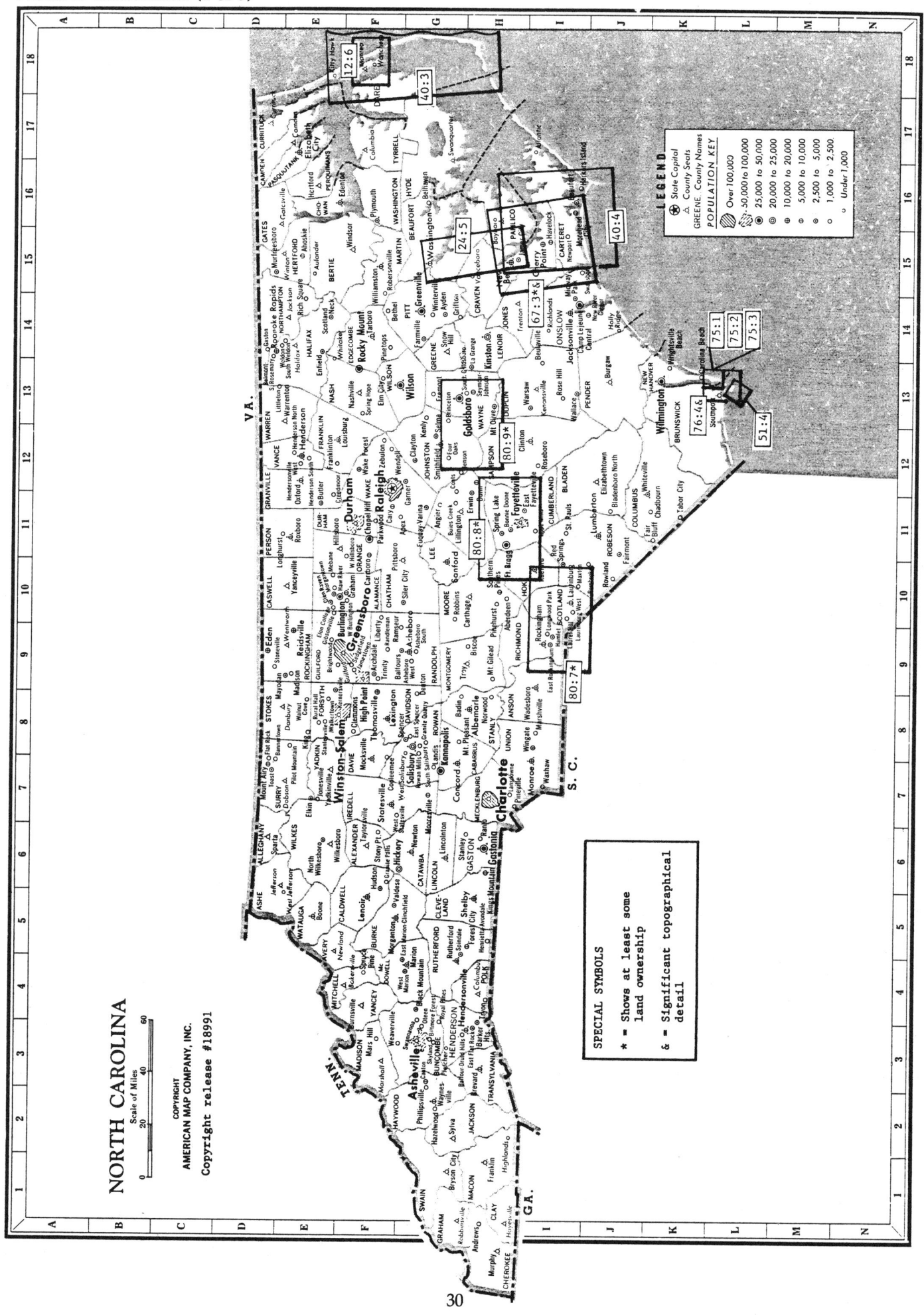

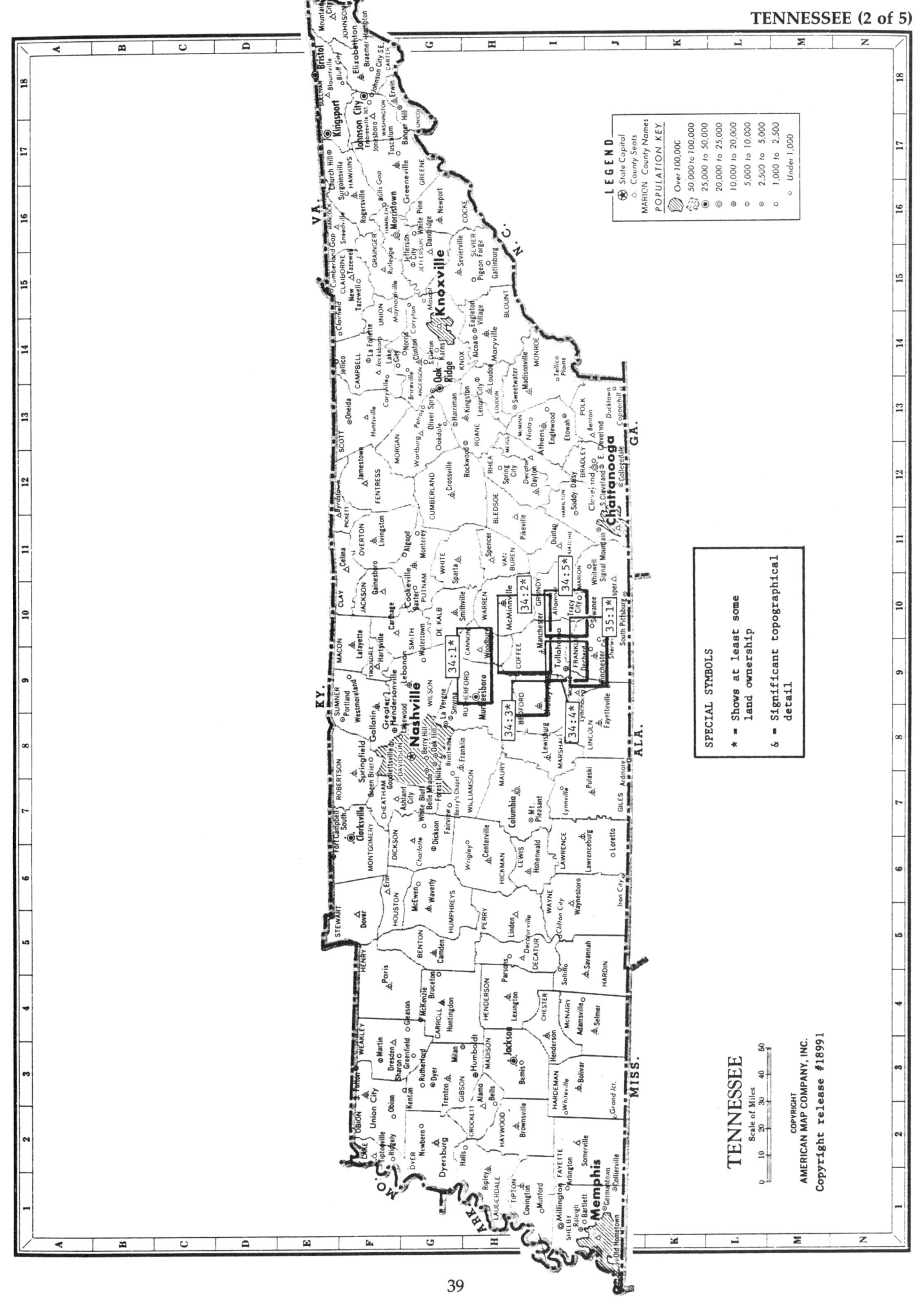

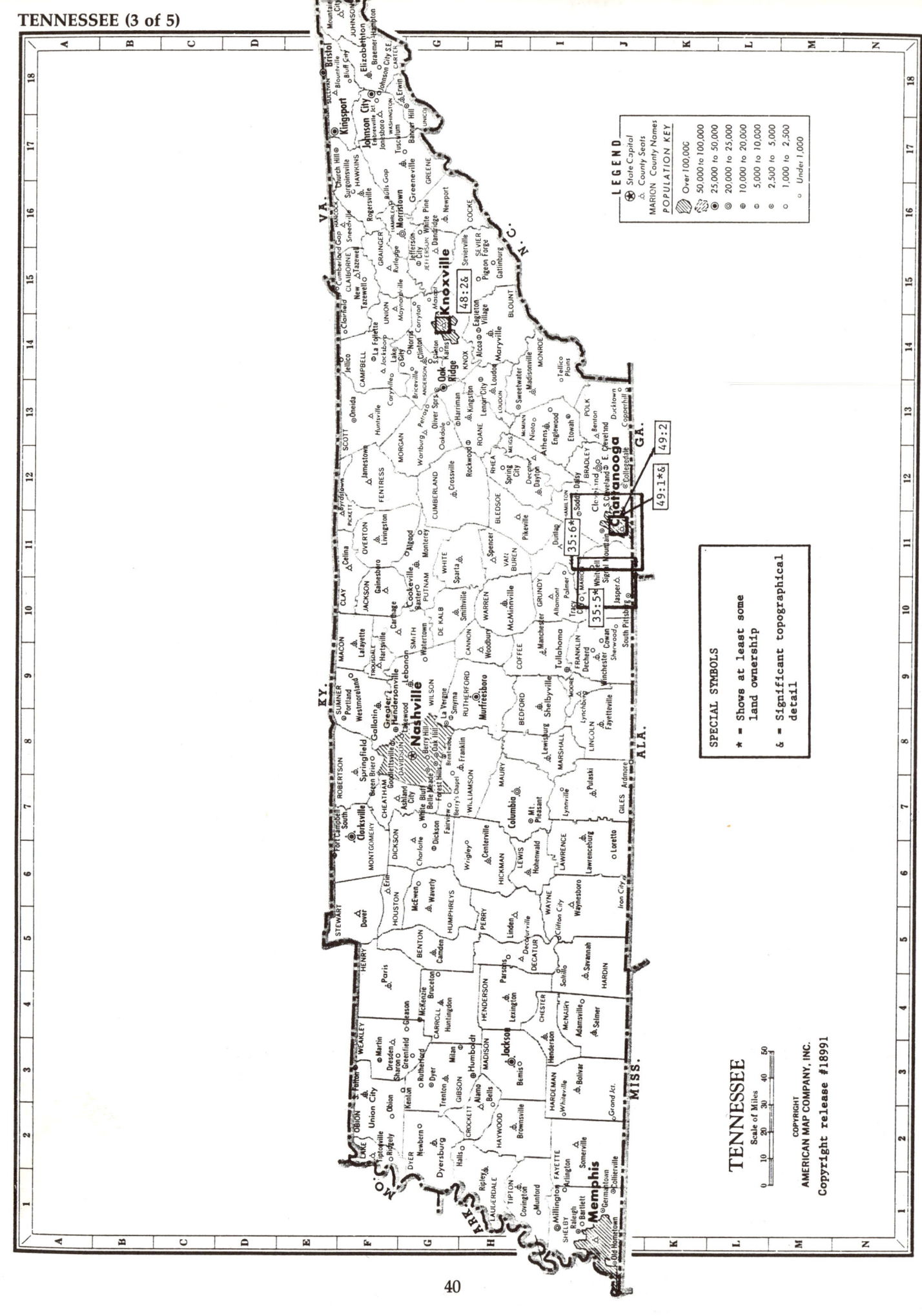

TENNESSEE (4 of 5)

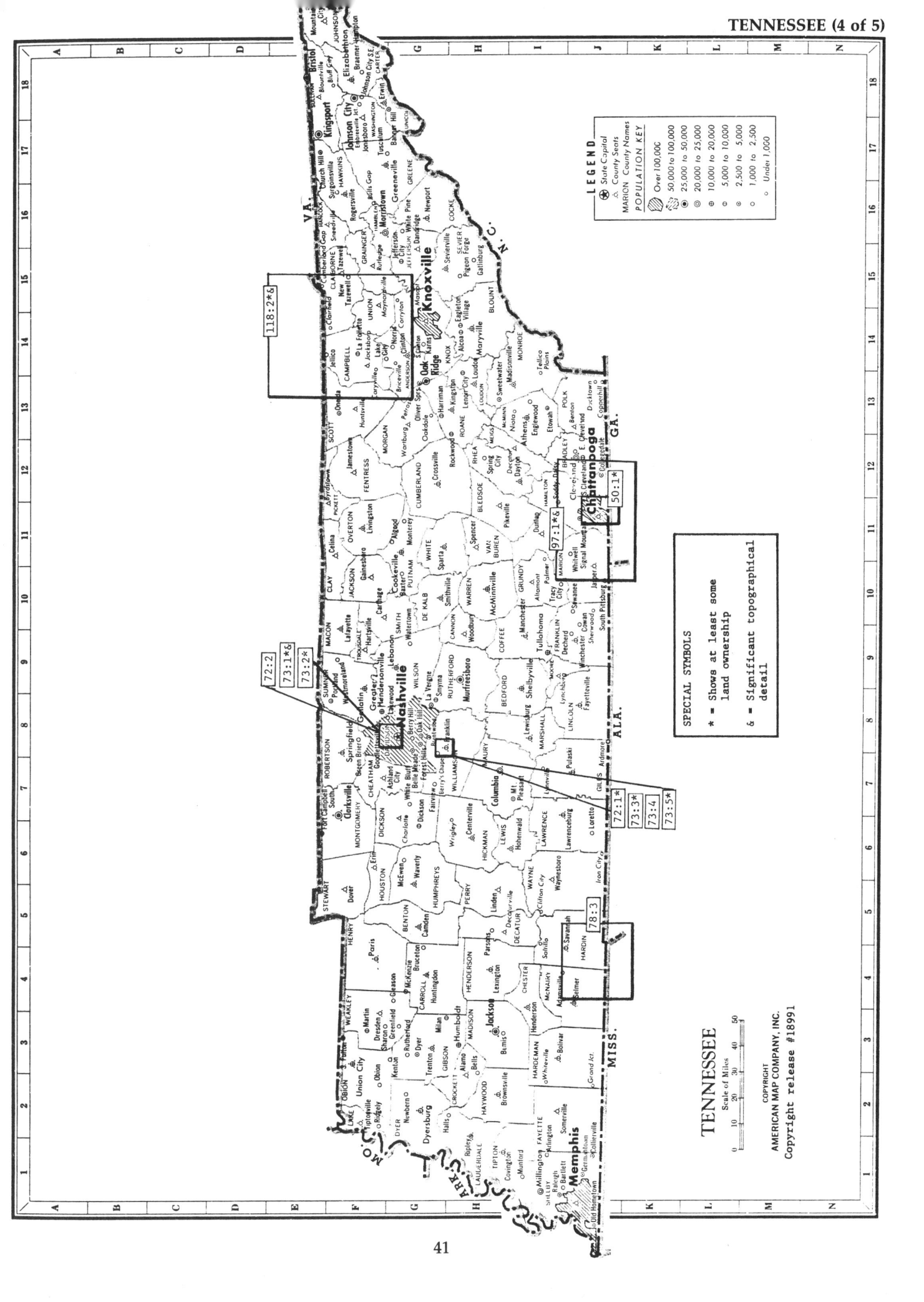

TENNESSEE (5 of 5)

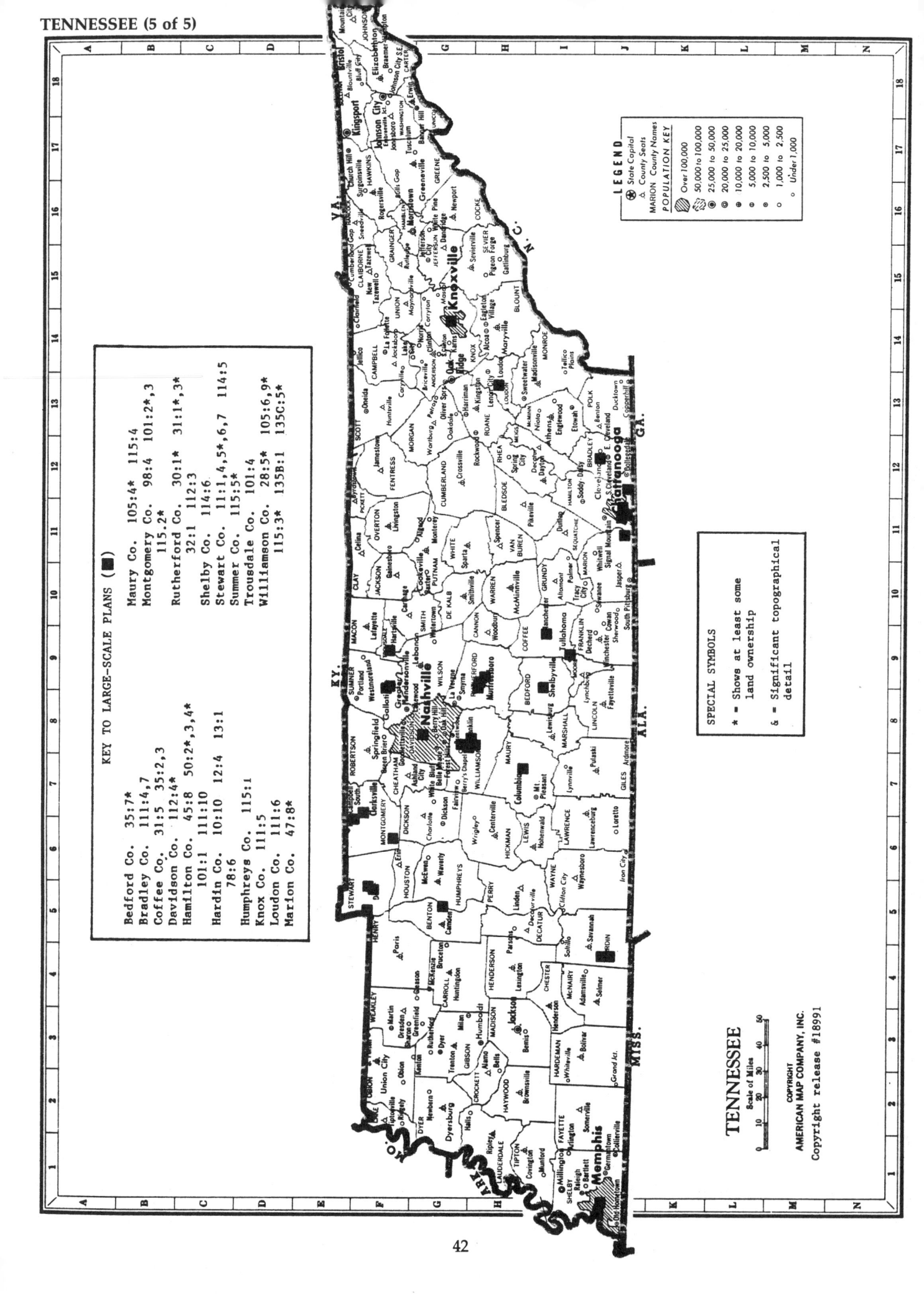

KEY TO LARGE-SCALE PLANS (■)

Bedford Co. 35:7*	Maury Co. 105:4* 115:4
Bradley Co. 111:4,7	Montgomery Co. 98:4 101:2*,3 115.2*
Coffee Co. 31:5 35:2,3	Rutherford Co. 30:1* 31:1*,3* 32:1 112:3
Davidson Co. 112:4*	Shelby Co. 114:6
Hamilton Co. 45:8 50:2*,3,4* 101:1 111:10	Stewart Co. 11:1,4,5*,6,7 114:5
Hardin Co. 10:10 12:4 13:1 78:6	Sumner Co. 115:5*
Humphreys Co. 115:1	Trousdale Co. 101:4
Knox Co. 111:5	Williamson Co. 28:5* 105:6,9* 115:3* 135B:1 135C:5*
Loudon Co. 111:6	
Marion Co. 47:8*	

SPECIAL SYMBOLS

* = Shows at least some land ownership

& = Significant topographical detail

LEGEND

⊛ State Capital
△ County Seats
MARION County Names

POPULATION KEY
- Over 100,000
- 50,000 to 100,000
- 25,000 to 50,000
- 20,000 to 25,000
- 10,000 to 20,000
- 5,000 to 10,000
- 2,500 to 5,000
- 1,000 to 2,500
- Under 1,000

TENNESSEE

Scale of Miles: 0 10 20 30 40 50

COPYRIGHT
AMERICAN MAP COMPANY, INC.
Copyright release #18991

TEXAS

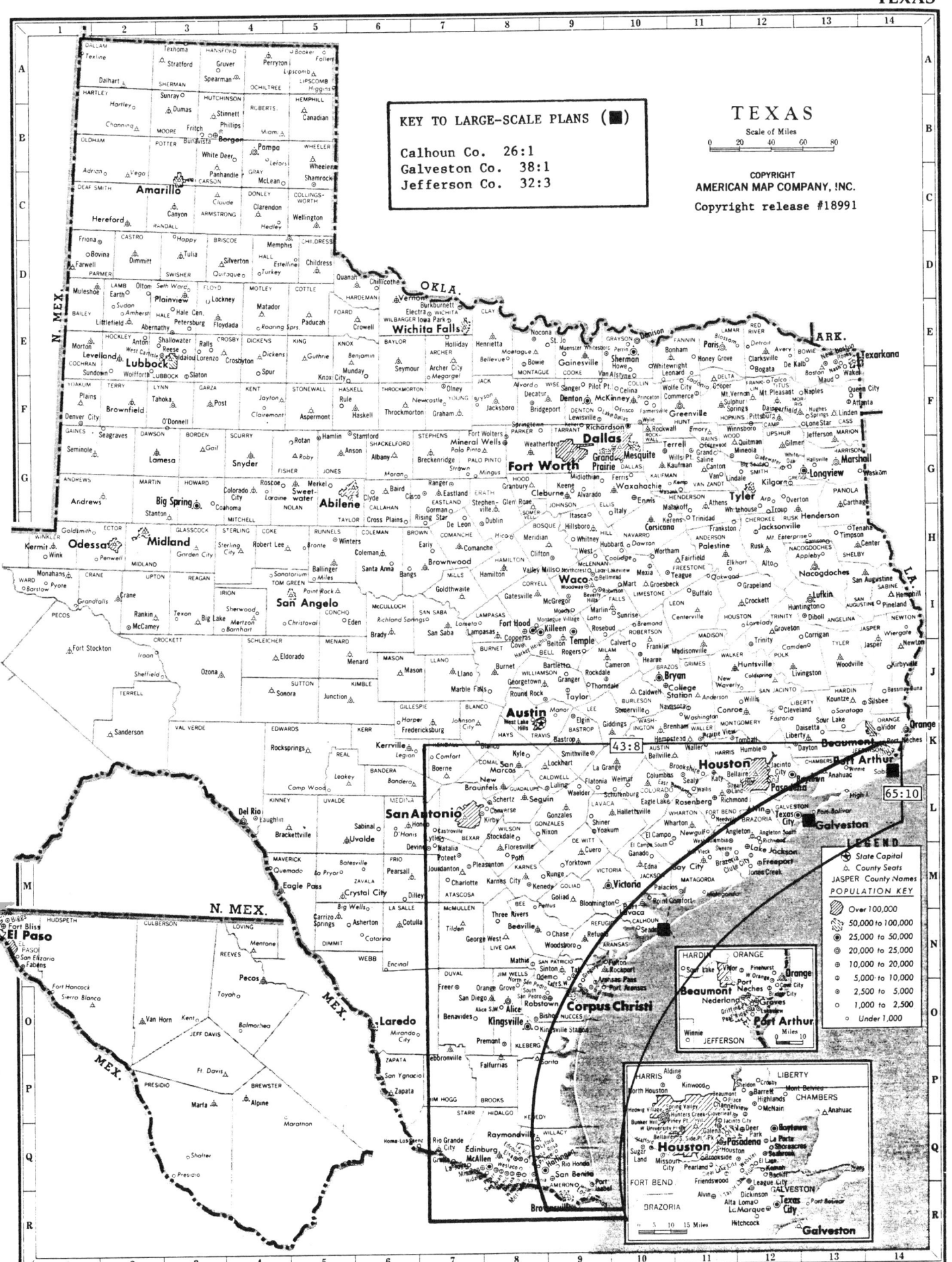

KEY TO LARGE-SCALE PLANS (■)

Calhoun Co. 26:1
Galveston Co. 38:1
Jefferson Co. 32:3

TEXAS
Scale of Miles
0 20 40 60 80

COPYRIGHT
AMERICAN MAP COMPANY, INC.
Copyright release #18991

LEGEND
- State Capital
- △ County Seats
- JASPER County Names

POPULATION KEY
- Over 100,000
- 50,000 to 100,000
- 25,000 to 50,000
- 20,000 to 25,000
- 10,000 to 20,000
- 5,000 to 10,000
- 2,500 to 5,000
- 1,000 to 2,500
- ○ Under 1,000

VIRGINIA (1 of 14)

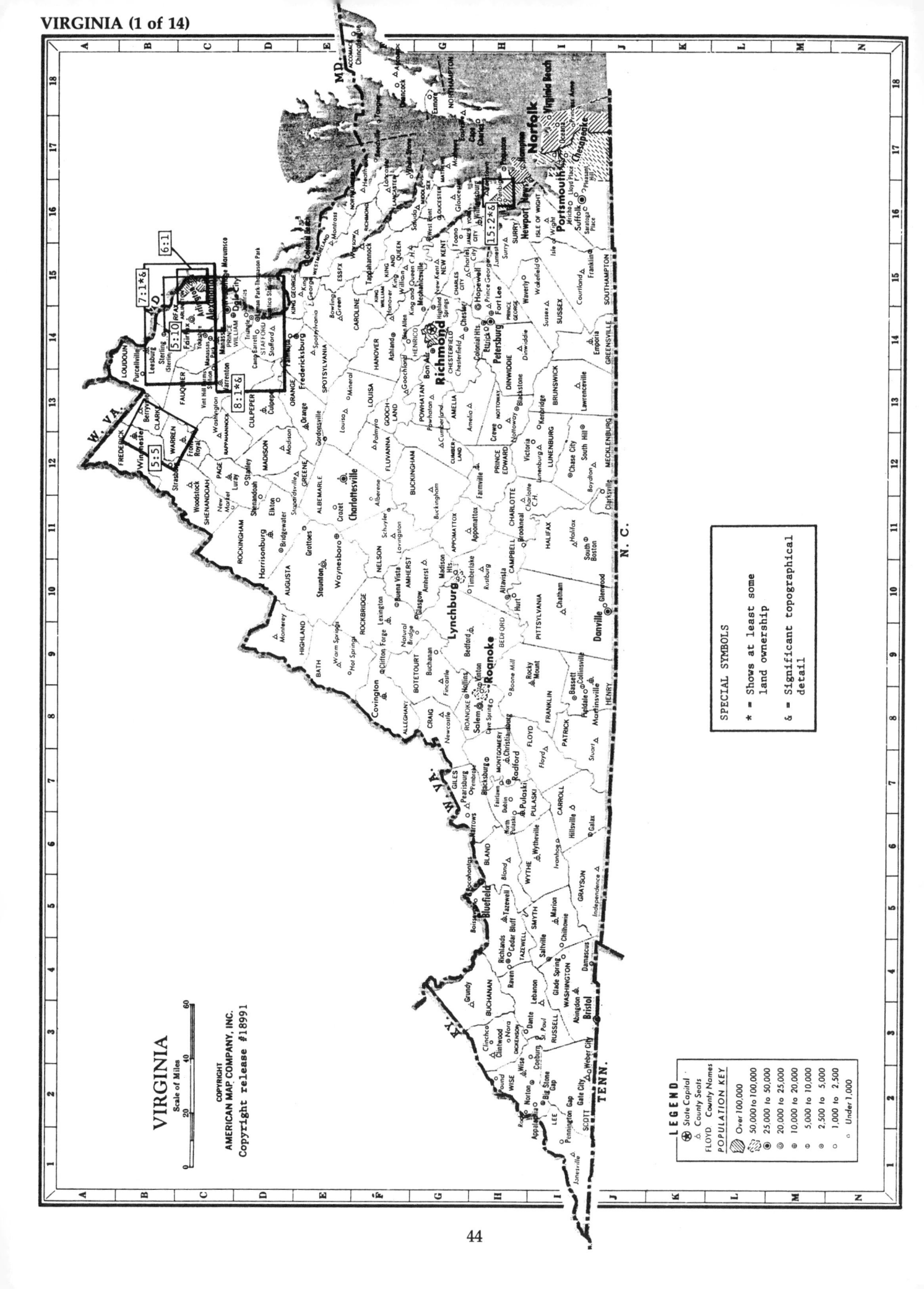

VIRGINIA (2 of 14)

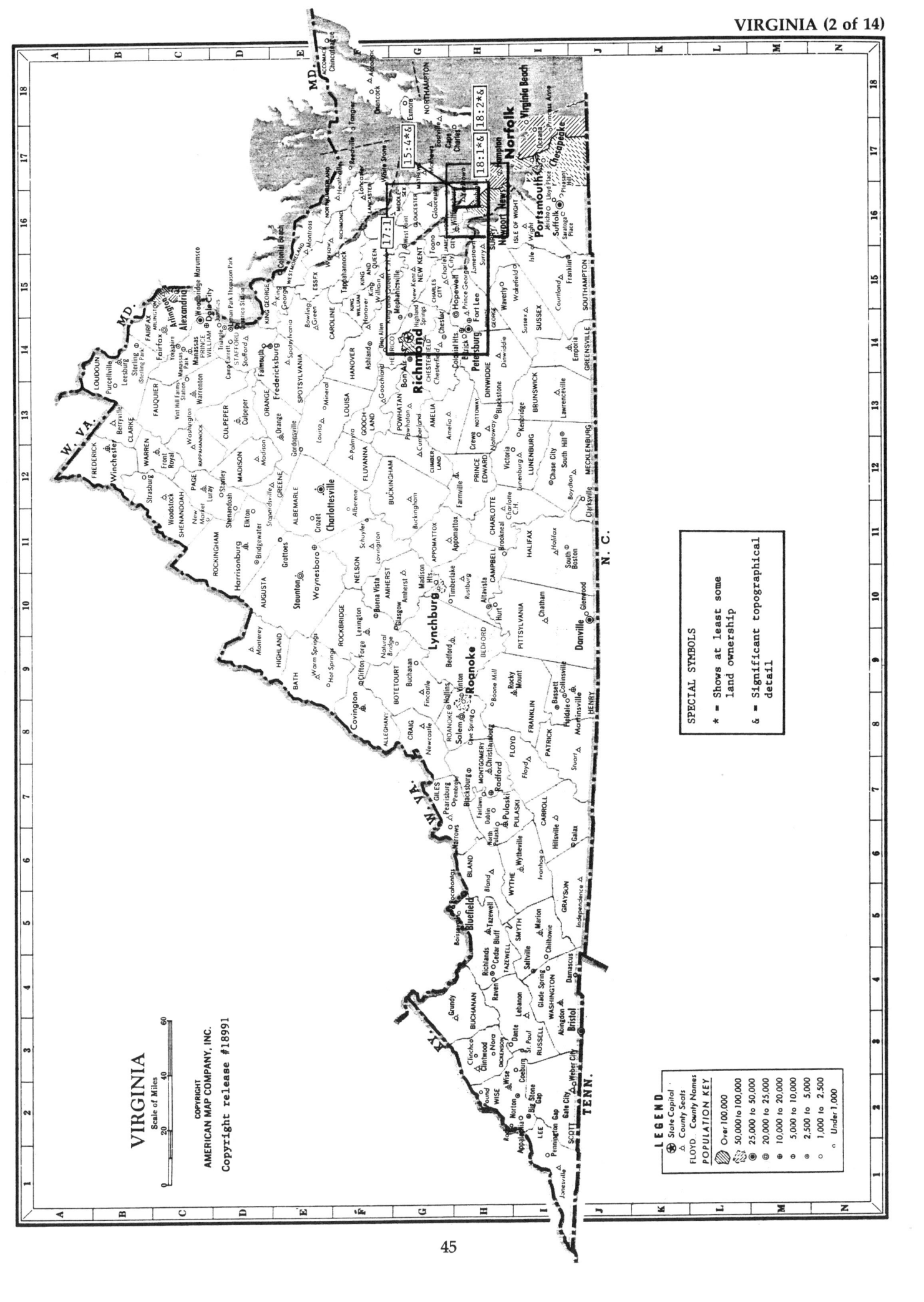

VIRGINIA
Scale of Miles
COPYRIGHT
AMERICAN MAP COMPANY, INC.
Copyright release #18991

LEGEND
- ⊕ State Capital
- △ County Seats
- FLOYD County Names
- **POPULATION KEY**
  - Over 100,000
  - 50,000 to 100,000
  - 25,000 to 50,000
  - 20,000 to 25,000
  - 10,000 to 20,000
  - 5,000 to 10,000
  - 2,500 to 5,000
  - 1,000 to 2,500
  - Under 1,000

SPECIAL SYMBOLS
- * = Shows at least some land ownership
- & = Significant topographical detail

VIRGINIA (3 of 14)

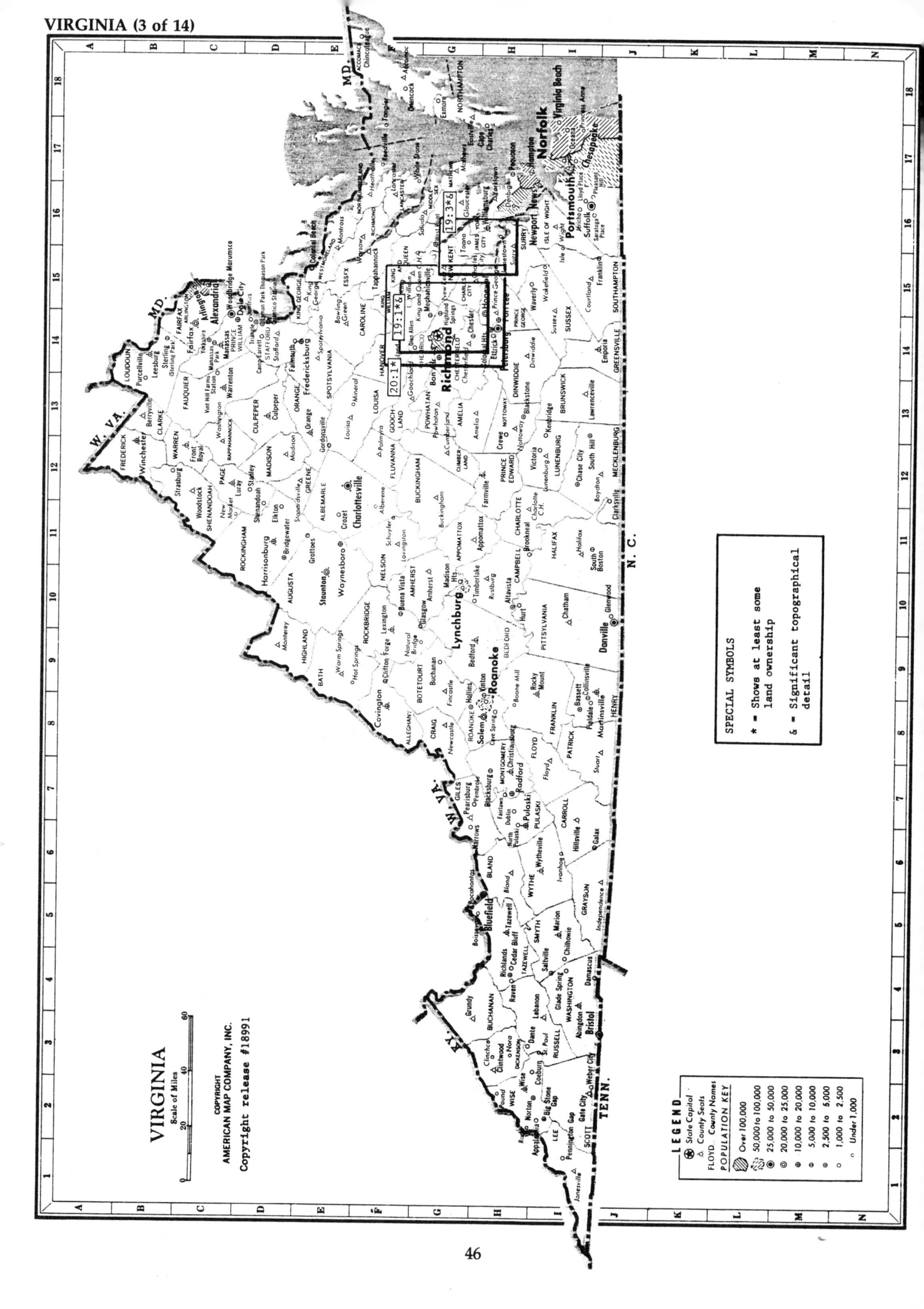

VIRGINIA (4 of 14)

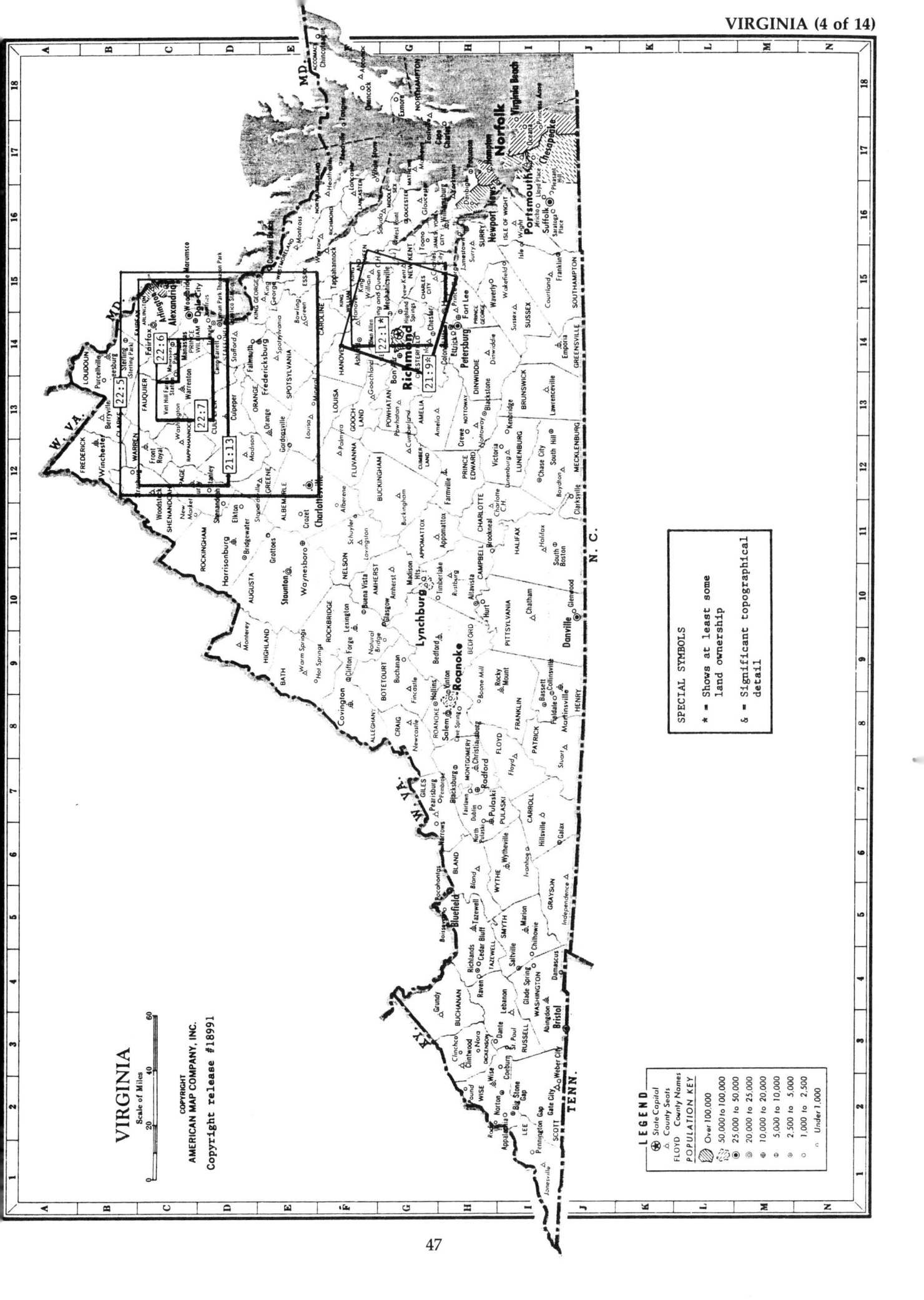

VIRGINIA (5 of 14)

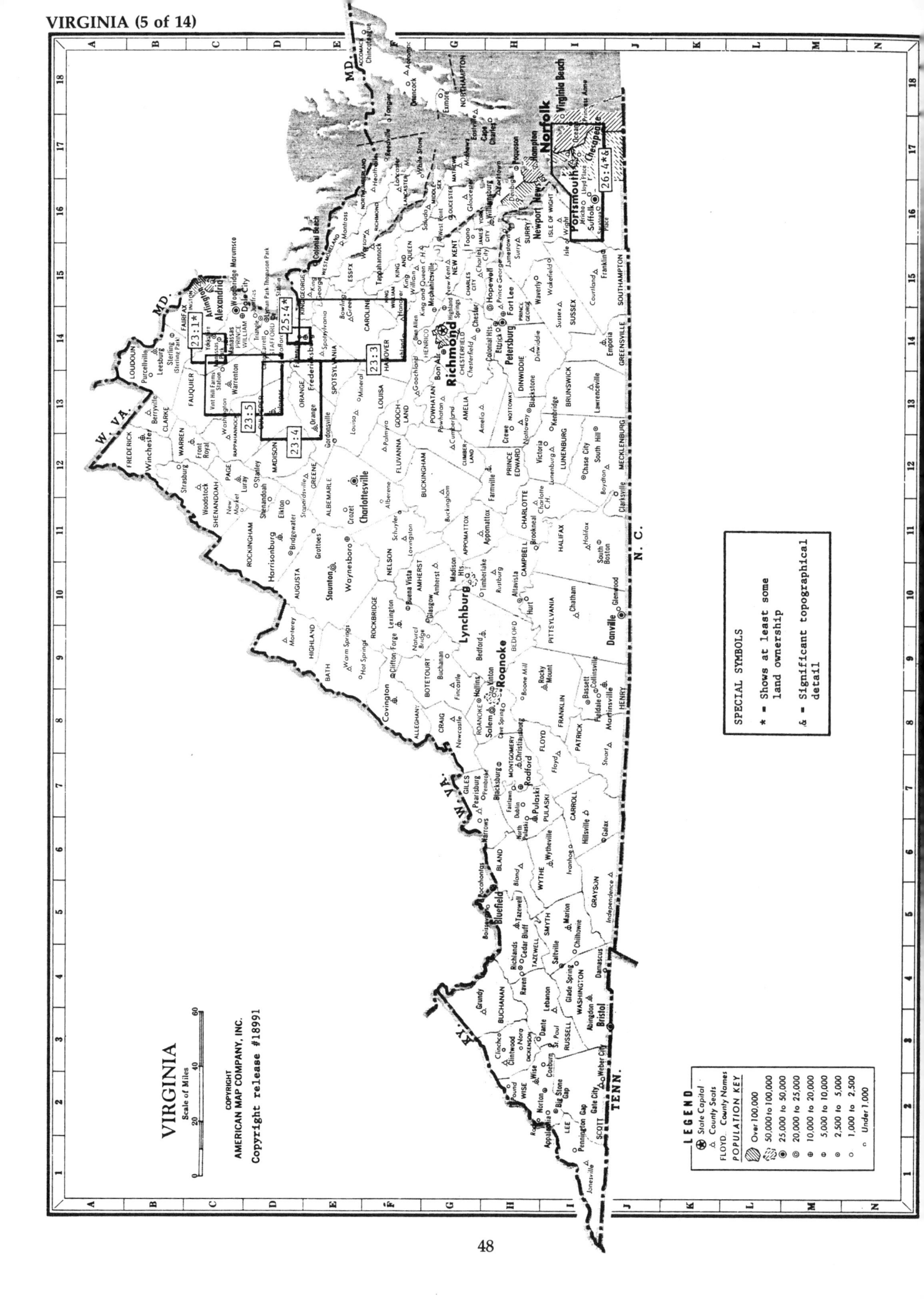

VIRGINIA (6 of 14)

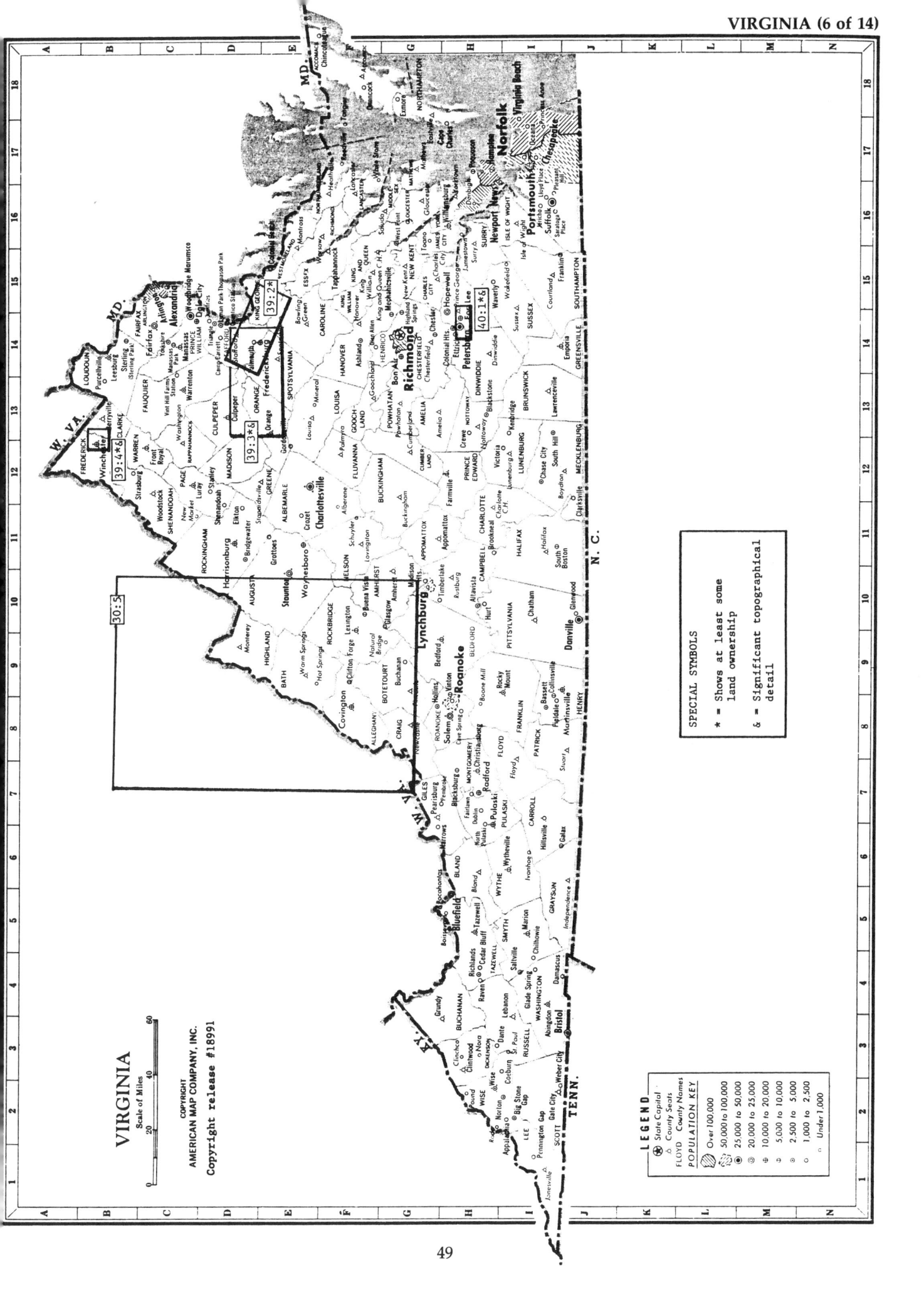

VIRGINIA (7 of 14)

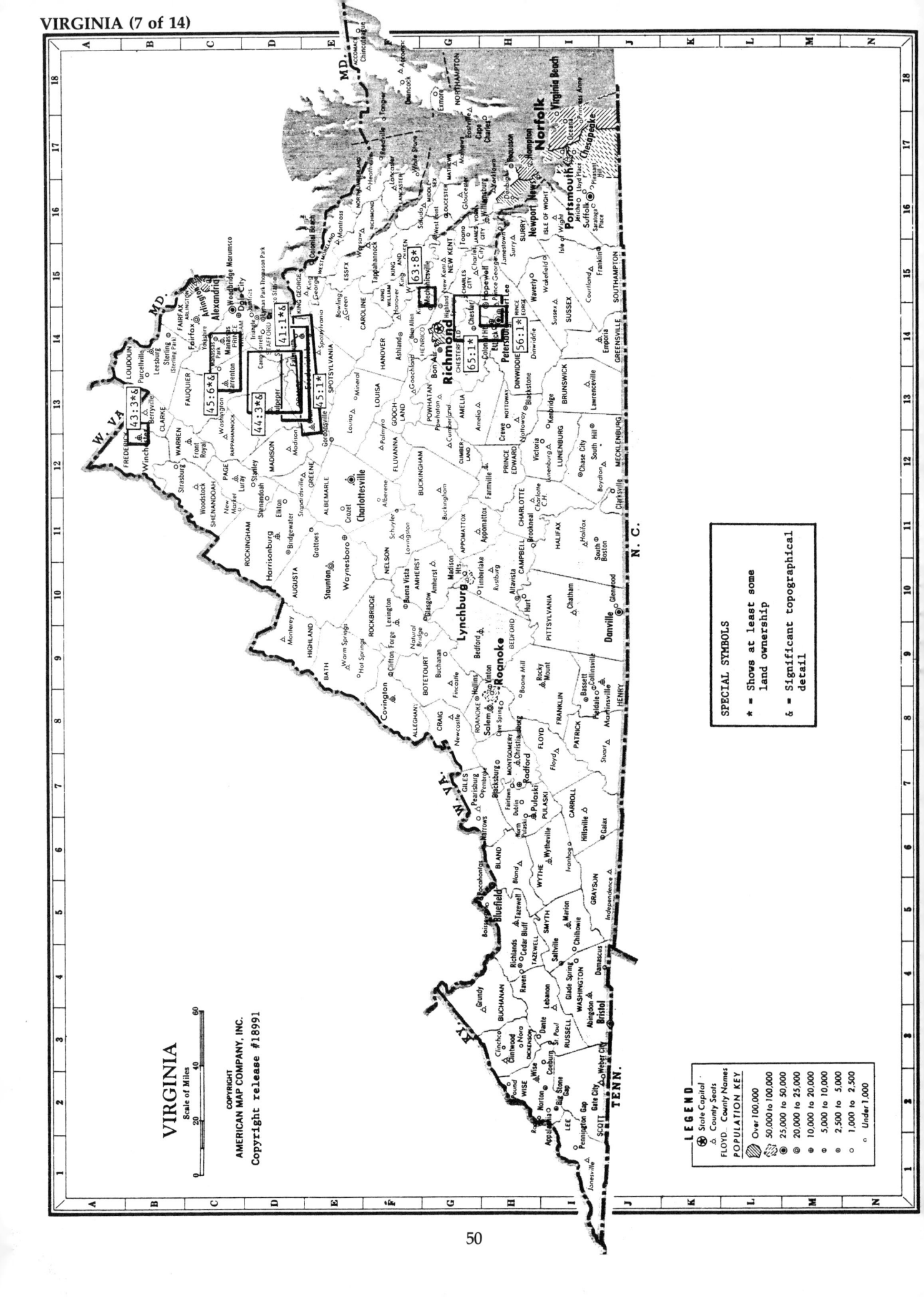

VIRGINIA (8 of 14)

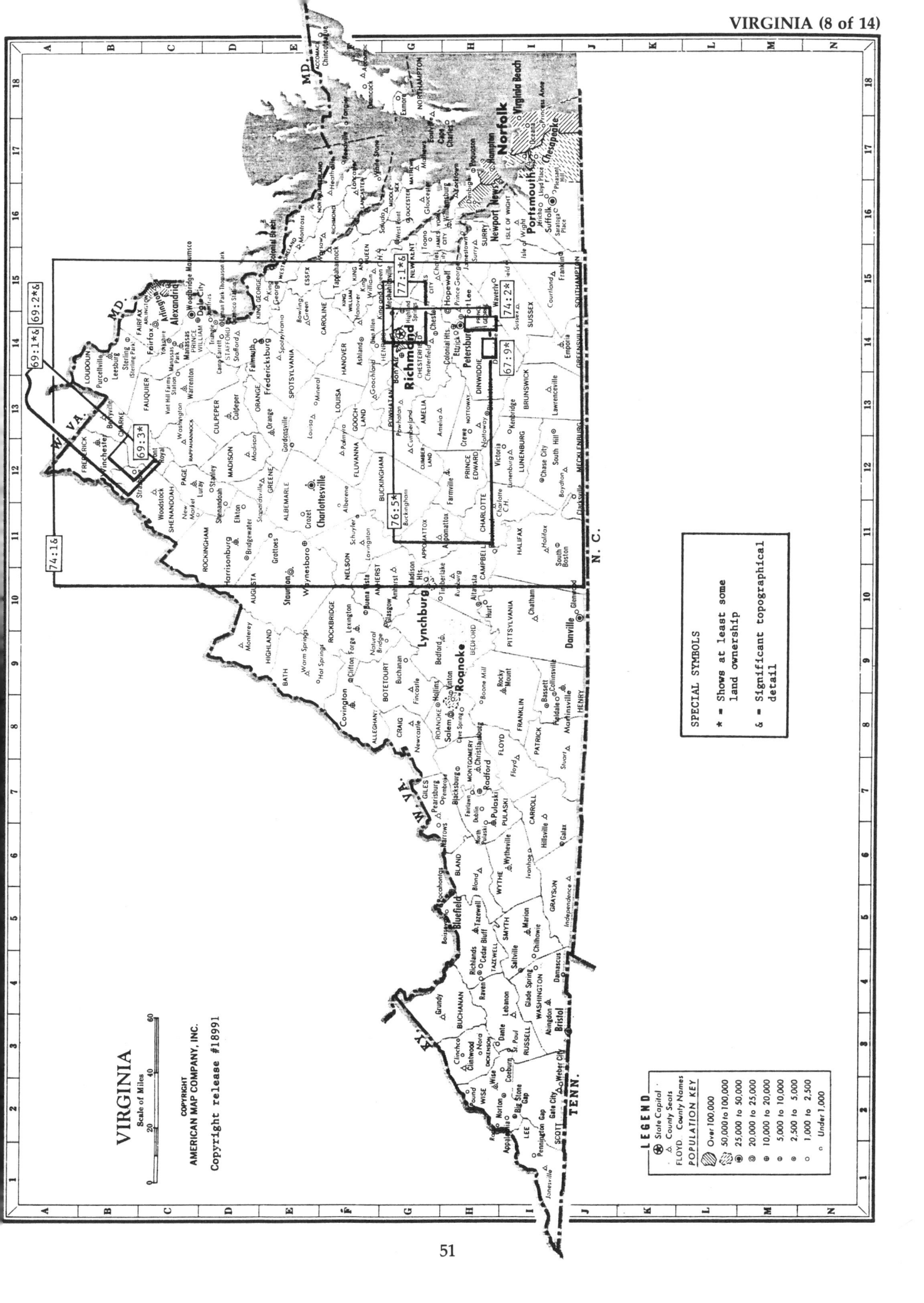

VIRGINIA (9 of 14)

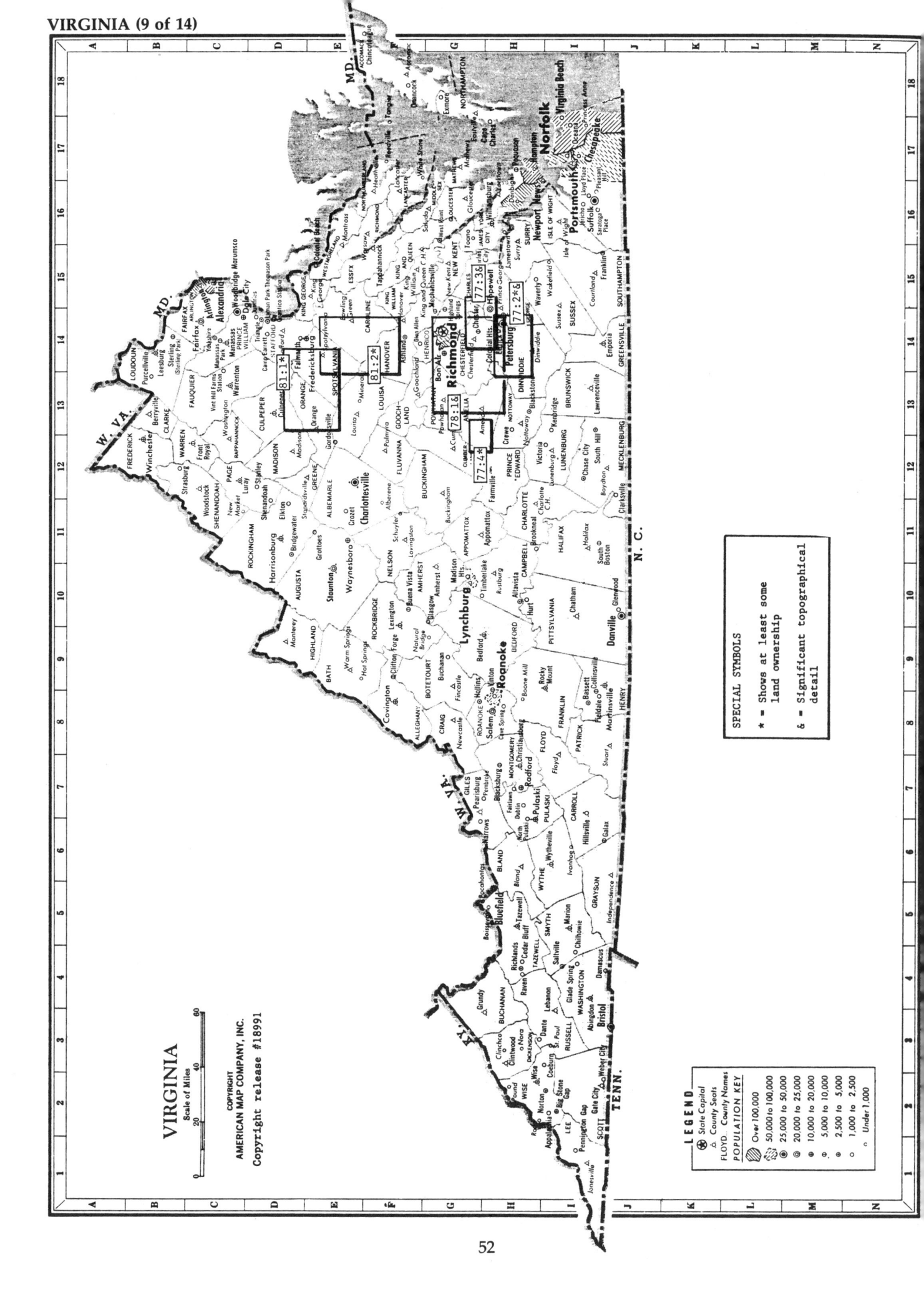

VIRGINIA

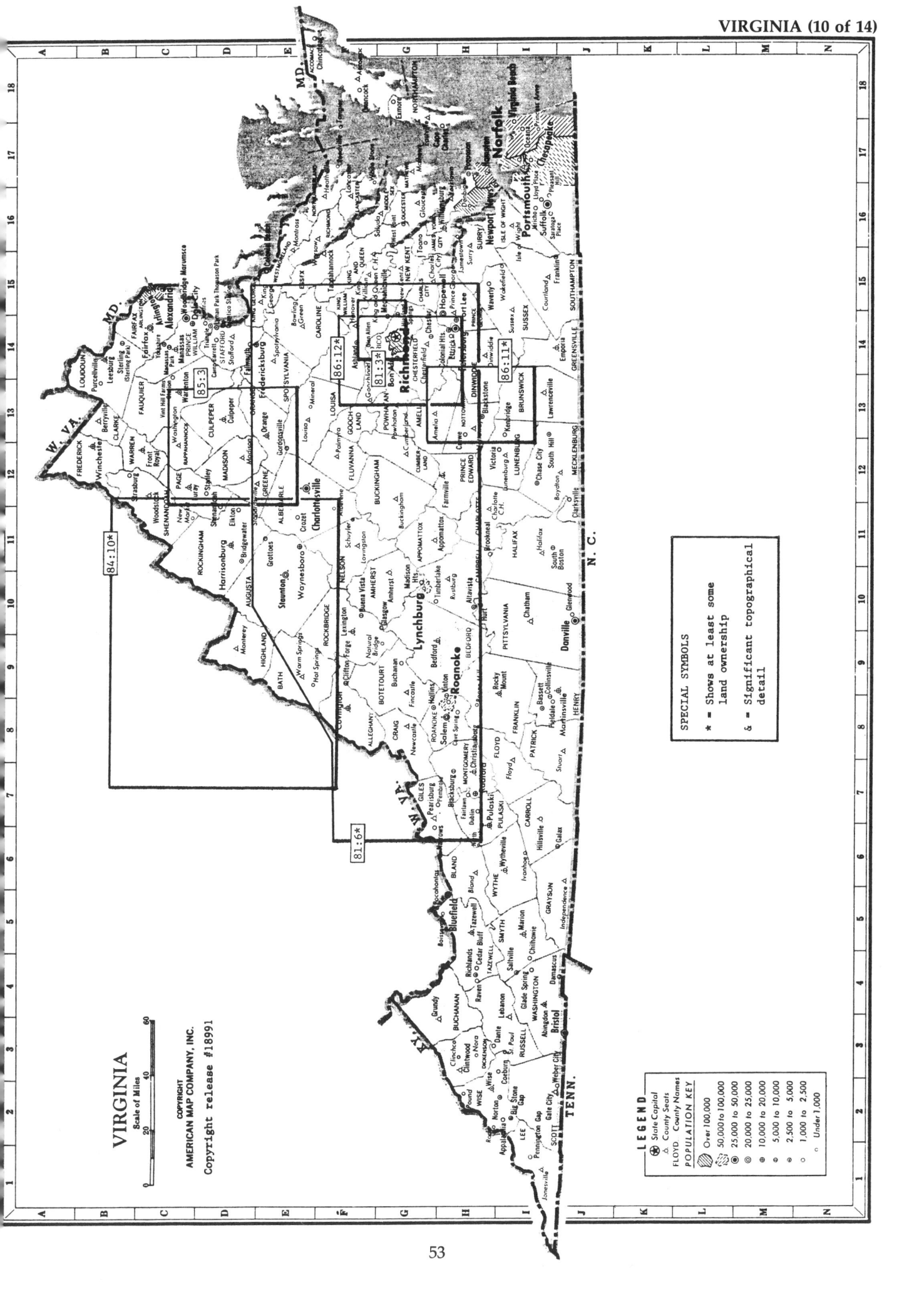

Scale of Miles

COPYRIGHT
AMERICAN MAP COMPANY, INC.
Copyright release #18991

LEGEND
- ⊛ State Capital
- ⊙ County Seats
- FLOYD County Names

POPULATION KEY
- Over 100,000
- 50,000 to 100,000
- 25,000 to 50,000
- 20,000 to 25,000
- 10,000 to 20,000
- 5,000 to 10,000
- 2,500 to 5,000
- 1,000 to 2,500
- Under 1,000

SPECIAL SYMBOLS
- * = Shows at least some land ownership
- & = Significant topographical detail

VIRGINIA (11 of 14)

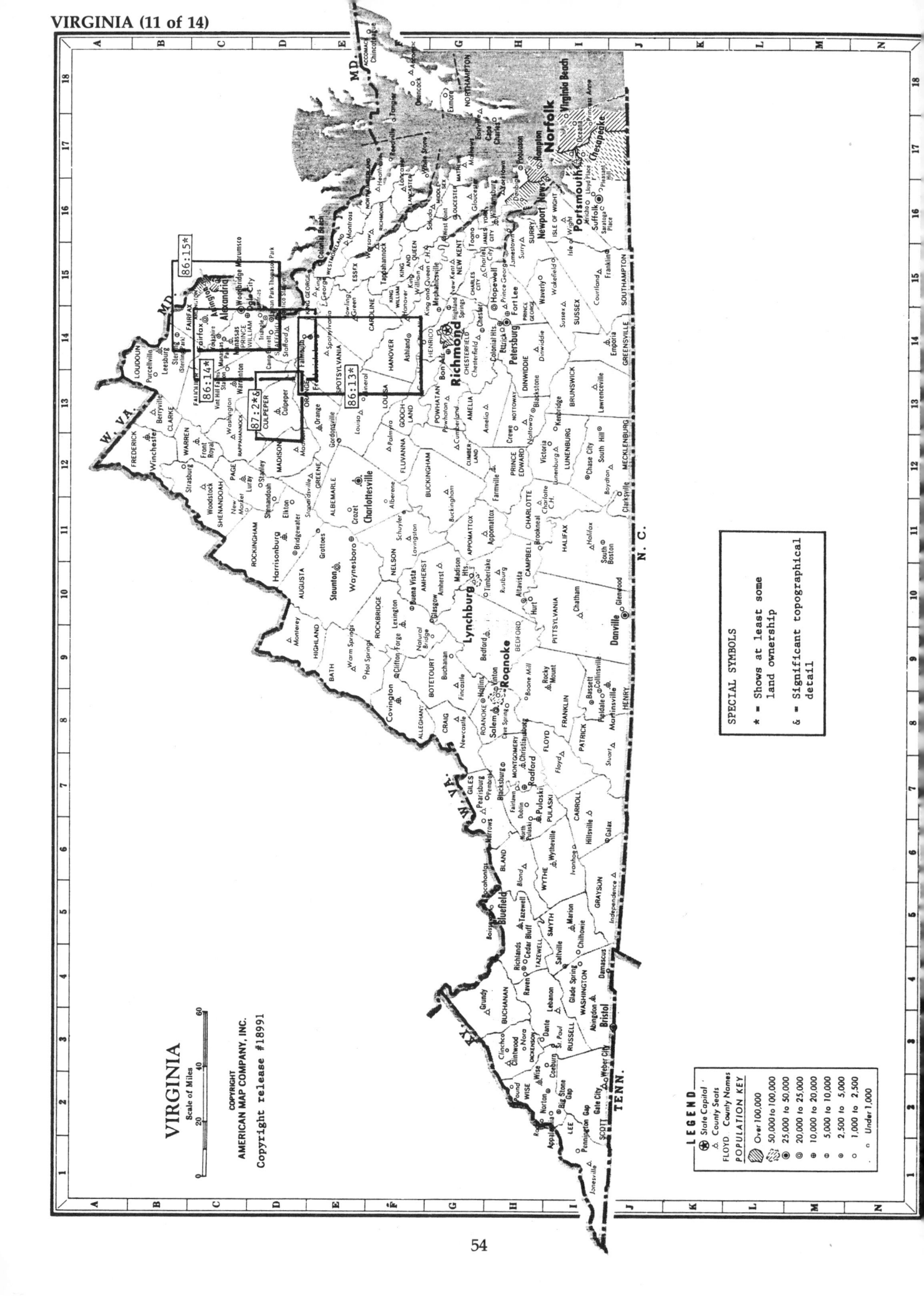

VIRGINIA (12 of 14)

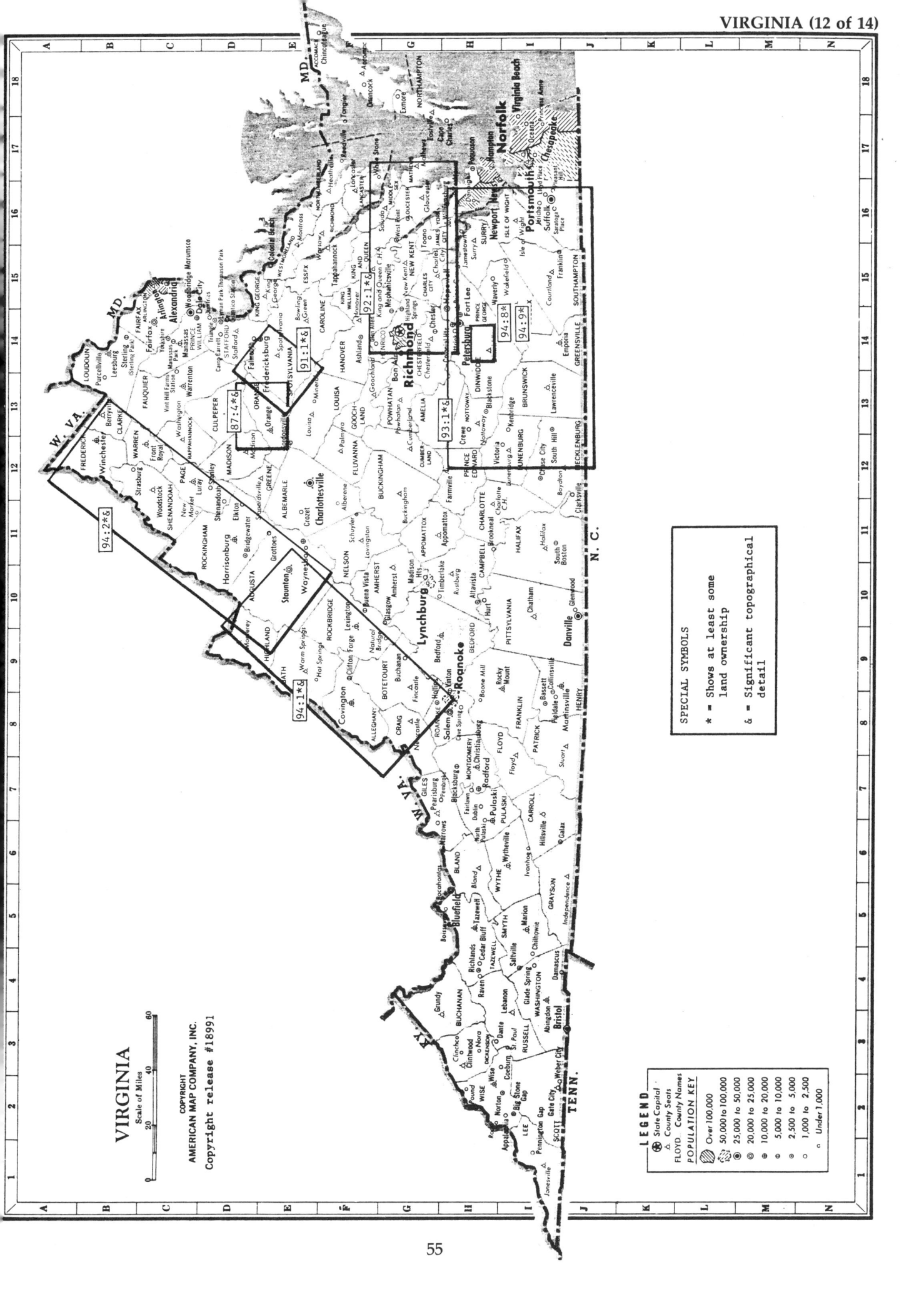

VIRGINIA (13 of 14)

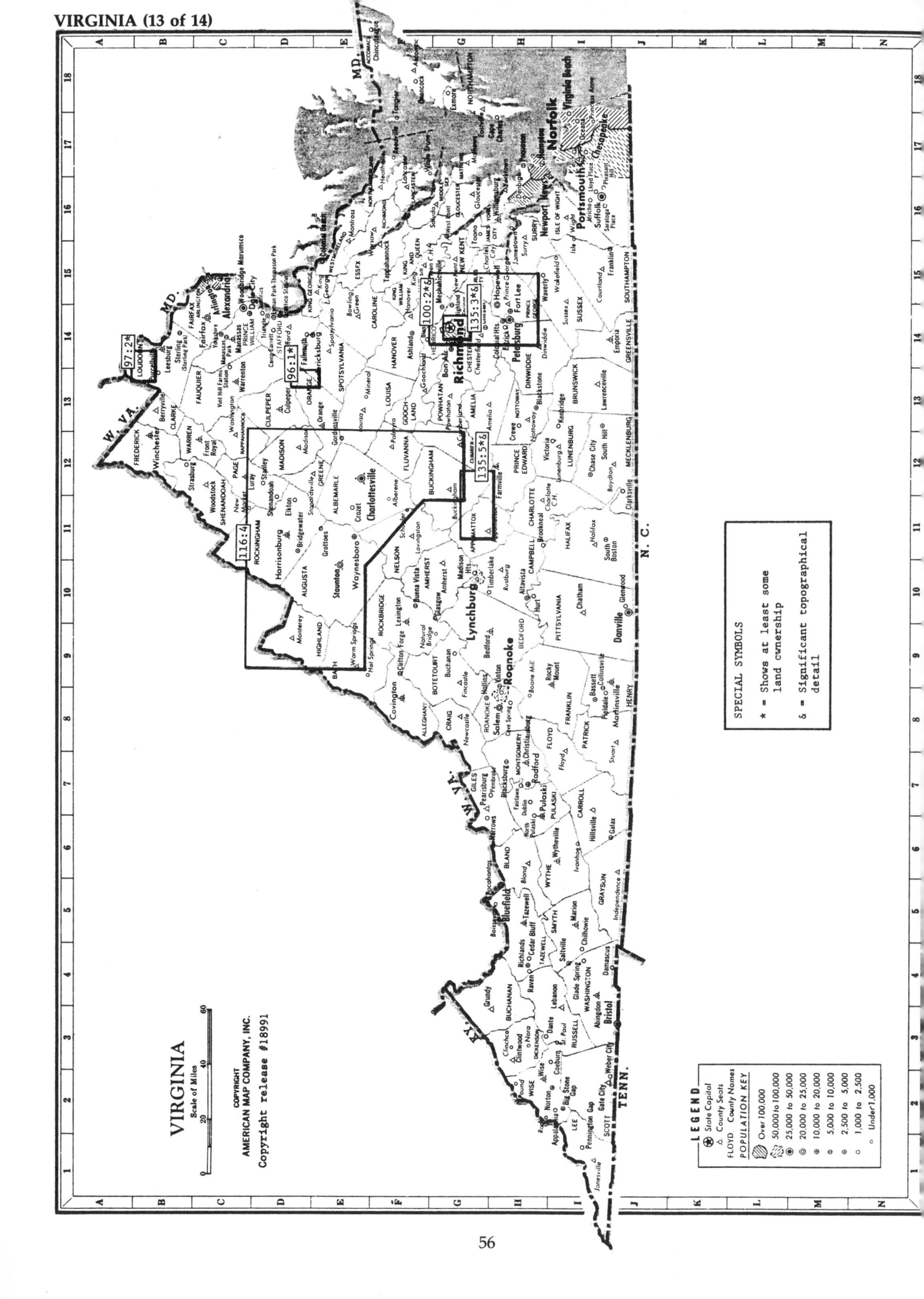

VIRGINIA (14 of 14)

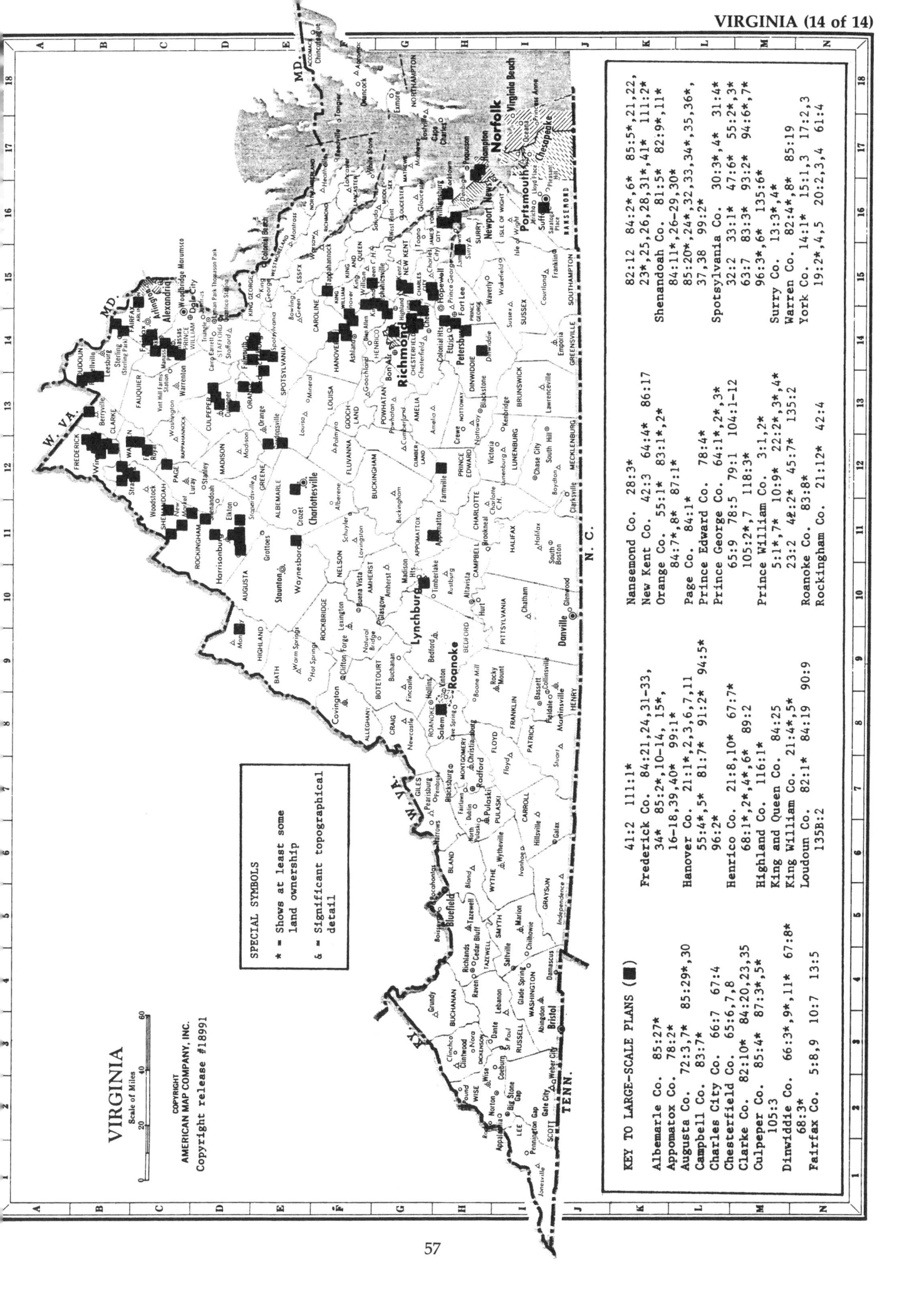

VIRGINIA

Scale of Miles 0 20 40 60

COPYRIGHT
AMERICAN MAP COMPANY, INC.
Copyright release #18991

SPECIAL SYMBOLS

* = Shows at least some land ownership

& = Significant topographical detail

KEY TO LARGE-SCALE PLANS (■)

Albemarle Co.	85:27*
Appomattox Co.	78:2*
Augusta Co.	72:3,7 85:29,30
Campbell Co.	83:7*
Charles City Co.	66:7 67:4
Chesterfield Co.	65:6,7,8 84:20,23,35
Clarke Co.	82:10 84:20,23,35
Culpeper Co.	85:4 87:3*,5*
Dinwiddie Co.	66:3*,9*,11 67:8*
	68:3*
Fairfax Co.	5:8,9 10:7 13:5
	41:2 111:1*
Frederick Co.	84:21,24,31-33,
	34* 85:2*,10-14, 15*,
	16-18,39,40* 99:1*
Hanover Co.	21:1*,2,3,6,7,11
	55:4,5* 81:7* 91:2* 94:5*
	96:2*
Henrico Co.	21:8,10* 67:7*
	68:1*,2*,4*,6* 89:2
Highland Co.	116:1*
King and Queen Co.	84:25
King William Co.	21:4*,5*
Loudoun Co.	82:1* 84:19 90:9
	135B:2
Nansemond Co.	28:3*
New Kent Co.	42:3 64:4* 86:17
Orange Co.	55:1* 83:1*,2*
	84:7*,8* 87:1*
Page Co.	84:1*
Prince Edward Co.	78:4*
Prince George Co.	64:1*,2*,3*
	65:9 78:5 79:1 104:1-12
	105:2*,7 118:3*
Prince William Co.	3:1,2*
	5:1*,7* 10:9* 22:2*,3*,4*
	23:2 42:2* 45:7* 135:2
Roanoke Co.	83:8*
Rockingham Co.	21:12* 42:4
	82:12 84:2*,6* 85:5*,21,22,
	23*,25,26,28,31*,41* 111:2*
Shenandoah Co.	81:5* 82:9*,11*
	84:11*,26-29,30*
	85:20*,24*,32,33,34*,35,36*,
	37,38 99:2*
Spotsylvania Co.	30:3*,4* 31:4*
	32:2 33:1* 47:6* 55:2*,3*
	63:7 83:3* 93:2* 94:6*,7*
	96:3*,6* 135:6*
Surry Co.	13:3*,4*
Warren Co.	82:4*,8* 85:19
York Co.	14:1* 15:1,3 17:2,3
	19:2*,4,5 20:2,3,4 61:4

WEST VIRGINIA

WEST VIRGINIA
Scale of Miles

COPYRIGHT
AMERICAN MAP COMPANY, INC.
Copyright release #18991

SPECIAL SYMBOLS
* = Shows at least some land ownership
& = Significant topographical detail

KEY TO LARGE-SCALE PLANS (■)

Berkeley Co. 82:2,7* 83:5*,6*
    84:12,15
Fayette Co. 9:1
Greenbrier Co. 135B:3
Hardy Co. 84:3*
Jefferson Co. 42:1   82:1,6*
    84:36* 85:6,7
Mineral Co. 54:2   84:4*,16,22
Morgan Co. 84:14*
Pendleton Co. 111:3
Randolph Co. 2:5,6*,7   84:5
Tyler Co. 85:9

58

VIRGINIA/MARYLAND THEATER (1 of 3)

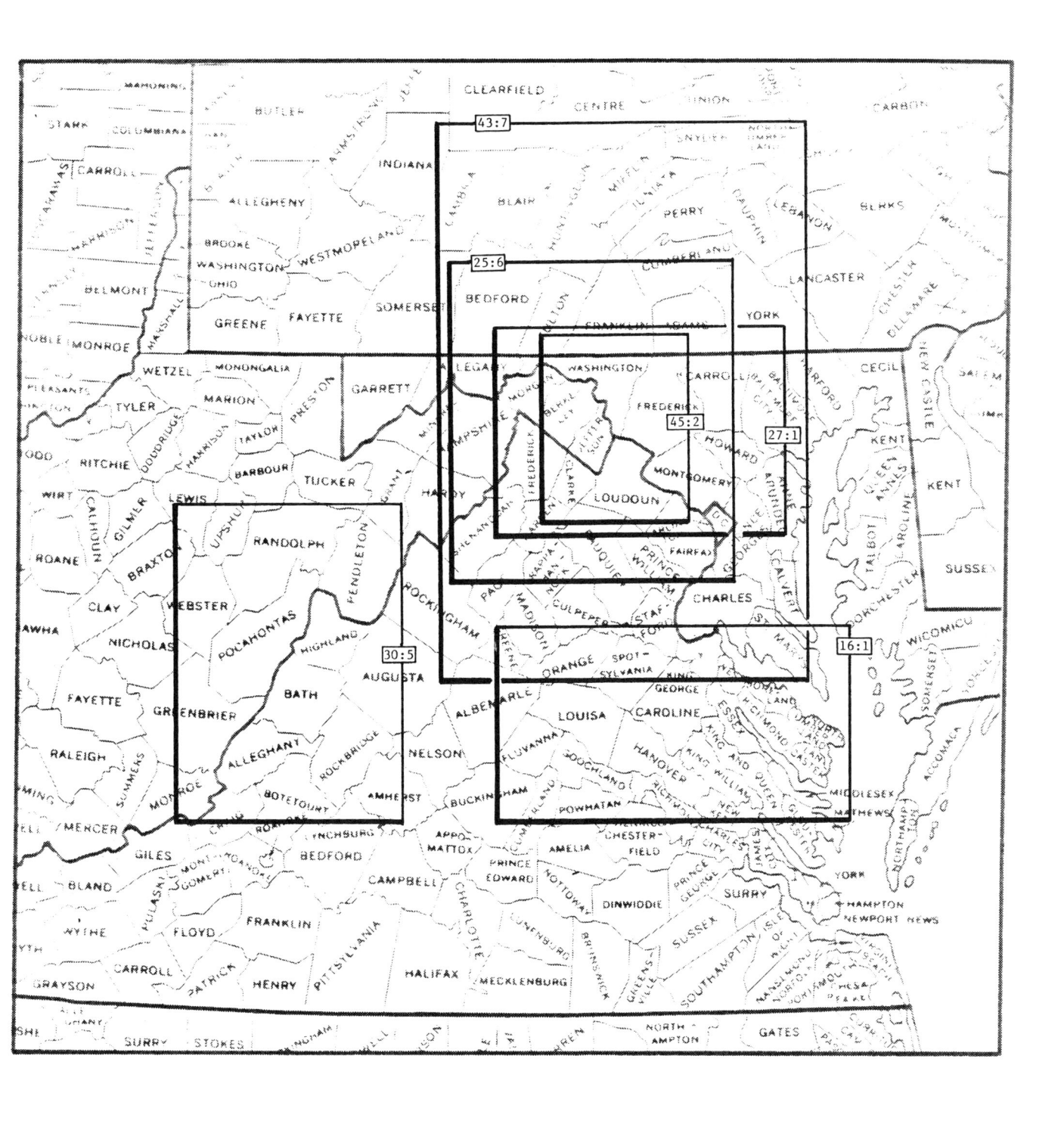

VIRGINIA/MARYLAND THEATER (2 of 3)

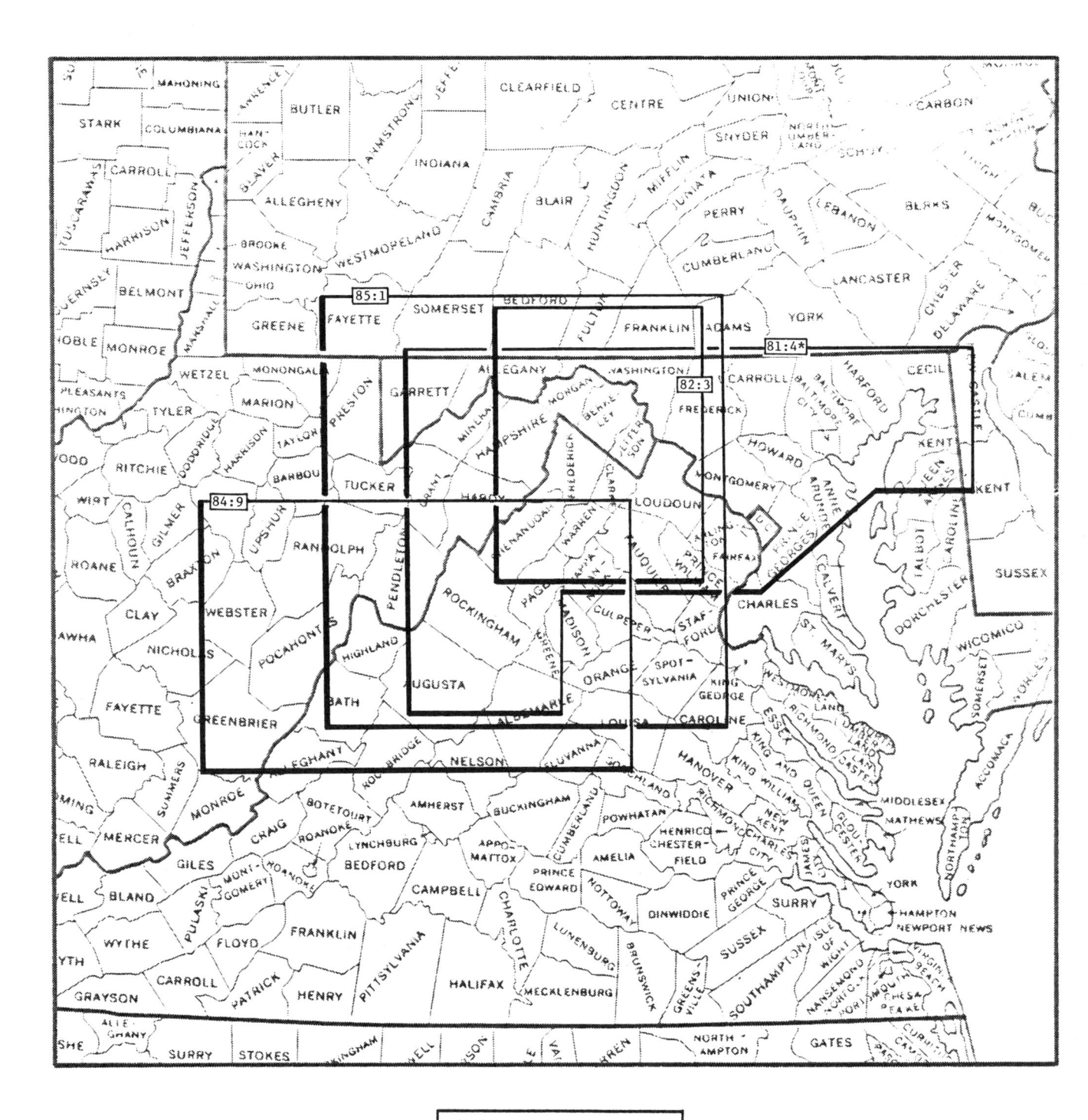

SPECIAL SYMBOLS

* = Shows at least some land ownership

& = Significant topographical detail

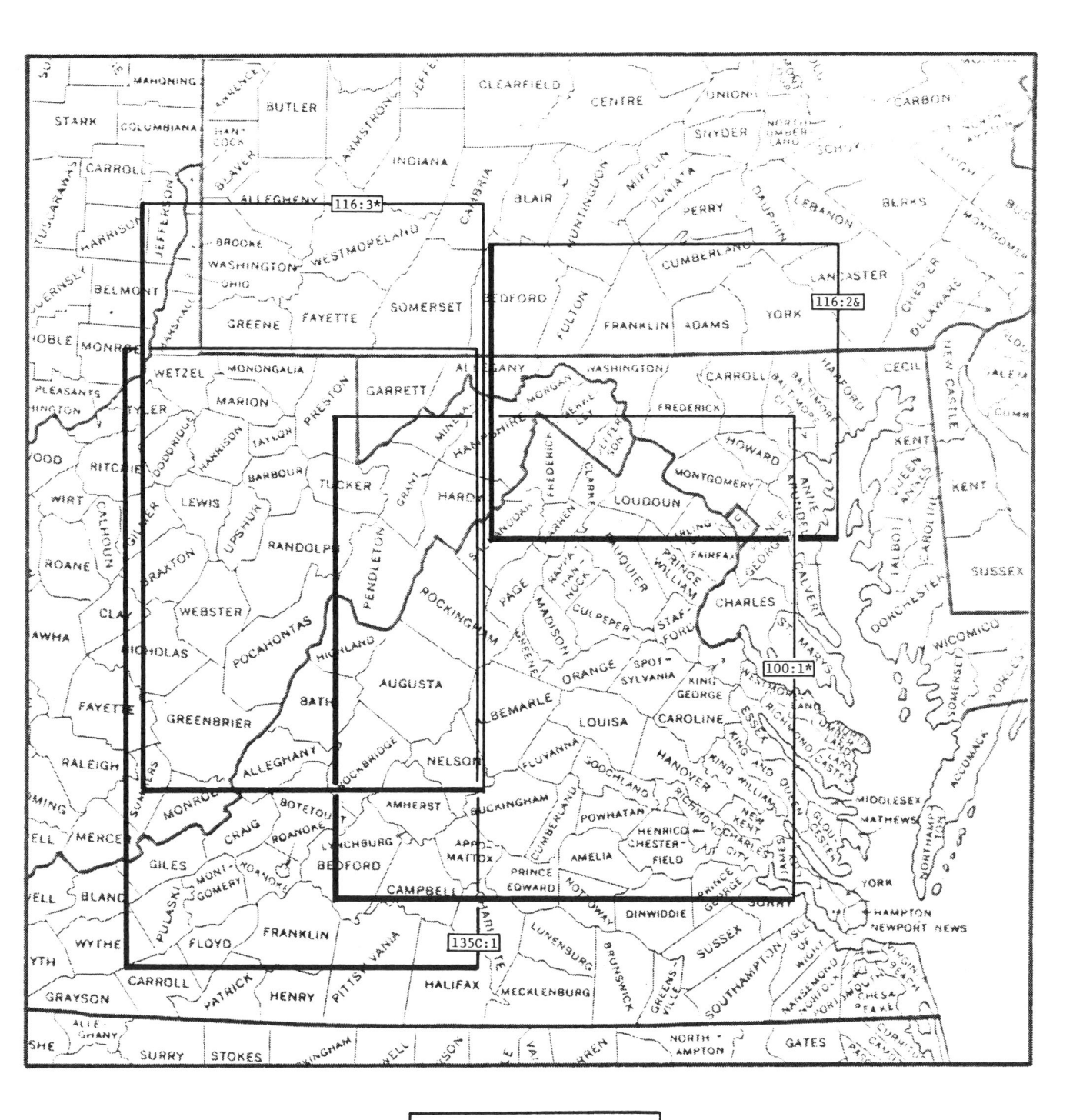

VIRGINIA/MARYLAND THEATER (3 of 3)

SPECIAL SYMBOLS

* = Shows at least some land ownership

& = Significant topographical detail

UNITED STATES (1 of 4)

SPECIAL SYMBOLS

* = Shows at least some land ownership
& = Significant topographical detail

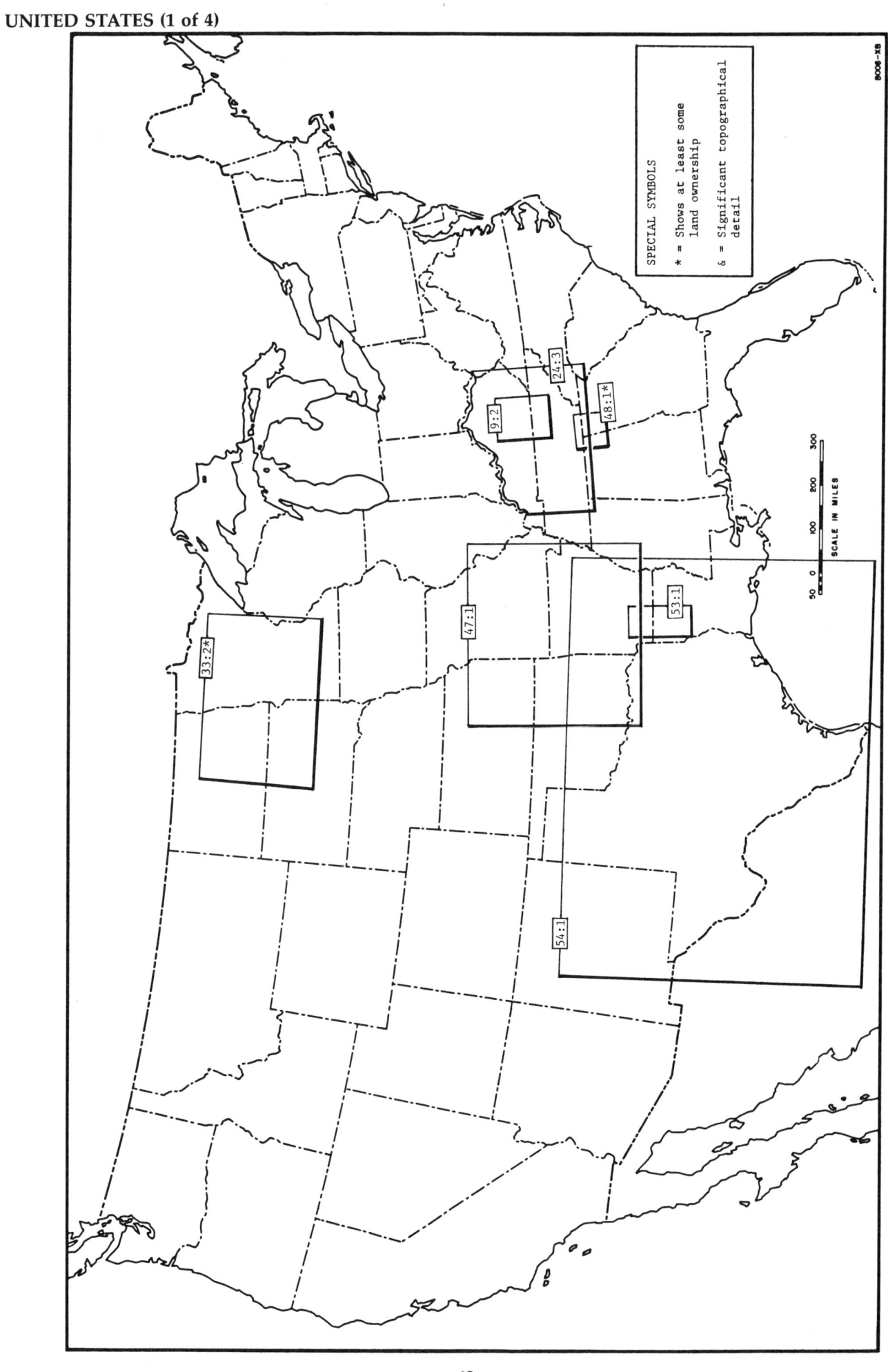

SCALE IN MILES
50 0 100 200 300

24:3
9:2
48:1*
47:1
53:1
33:2*
54:1

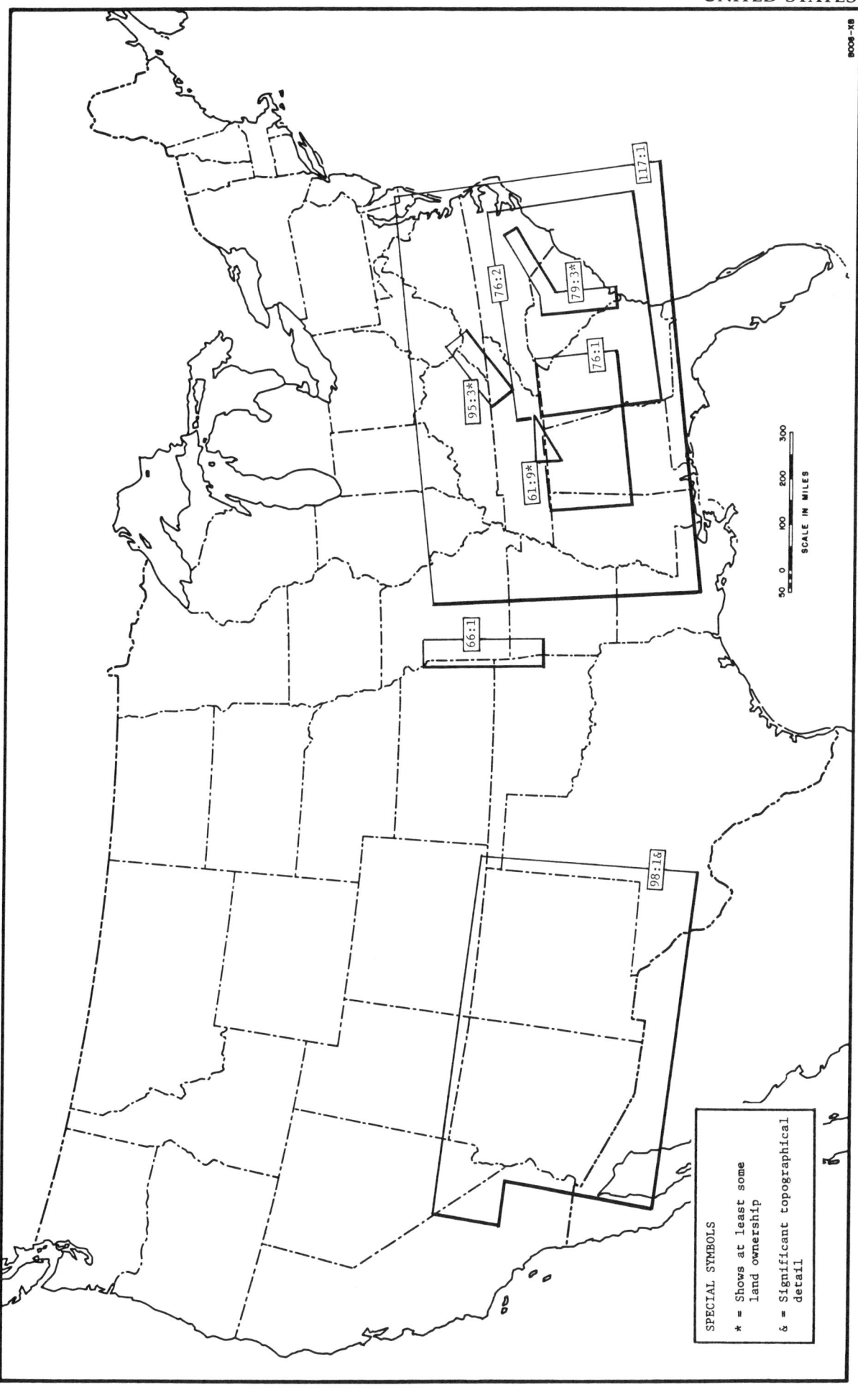

UNITED STATES (2 of 4)

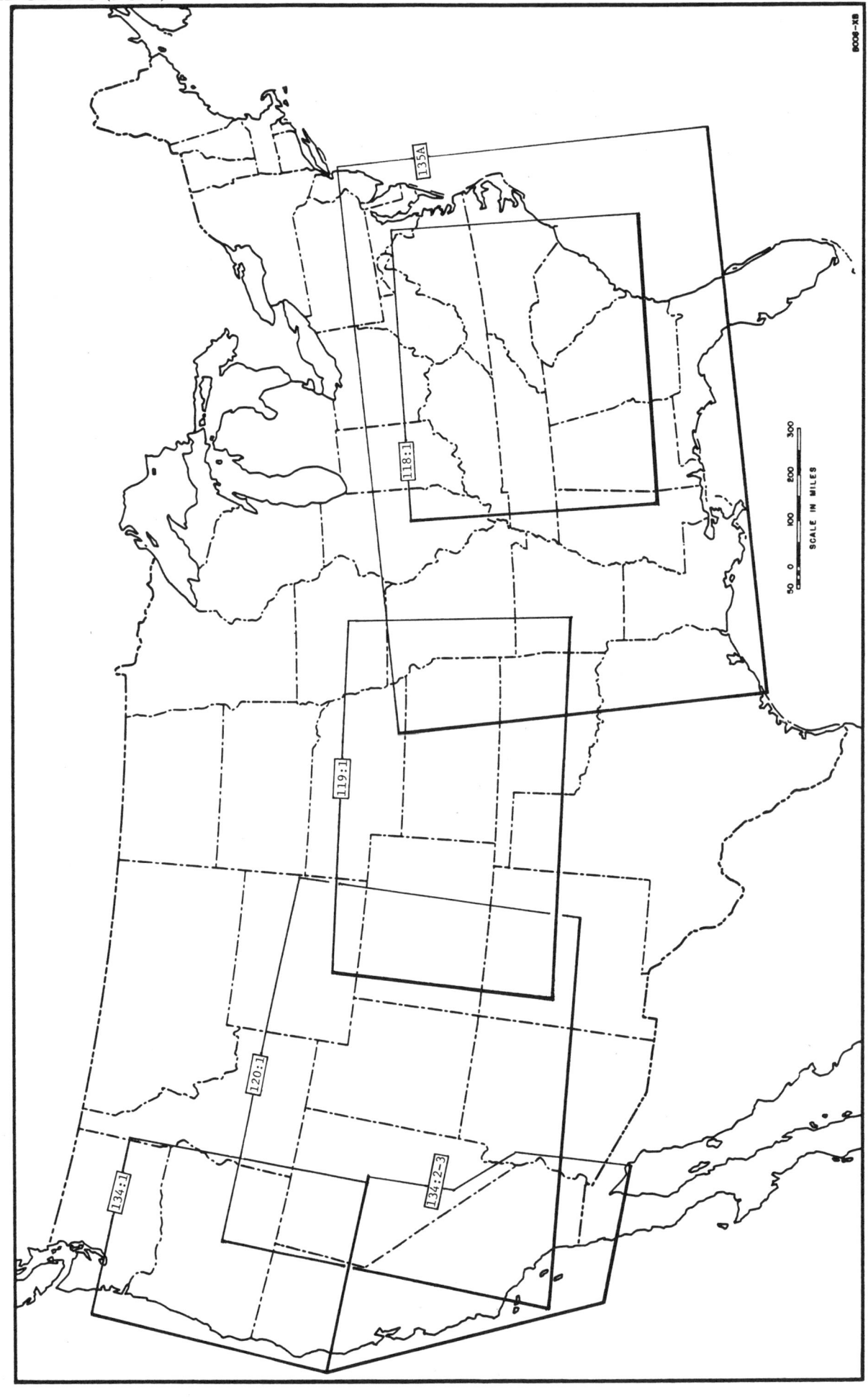

UNITED STATES (3 of 4)

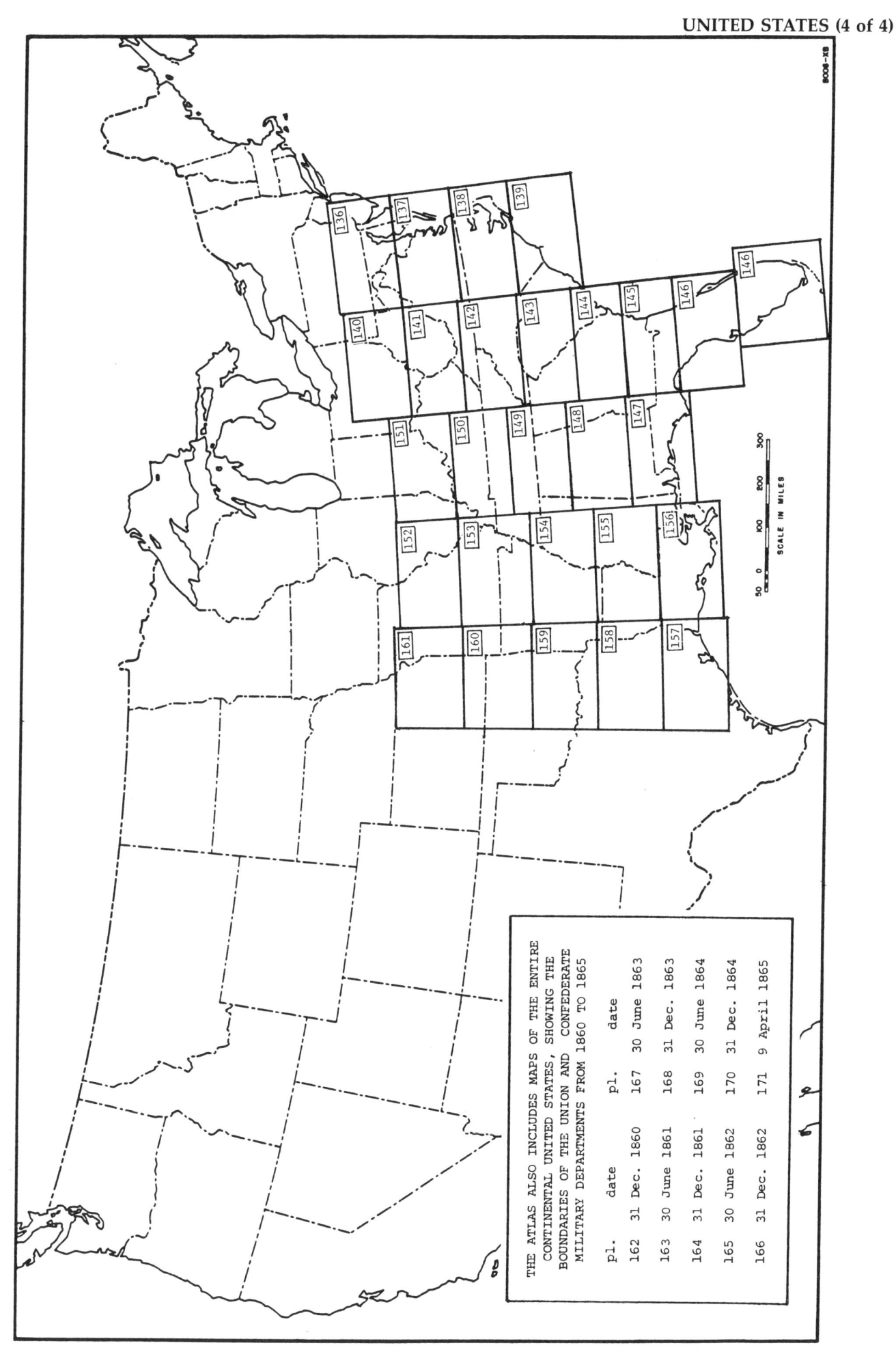

UNITED STATES (4 of 4)

THE ATLAS ALSO INCLUDES MAPS OF THE ENTIRE
CONTINENTAL UNITED STATES, SHOWING THE
BOUNDARIES OF THE UNION AND CONFEDERATE
MILITARY DEPARTMENTS FROM 1860 TO 1865

pl.	date	pl.	date
162	31 Dec. 1860	167	30 June 1863
163	30 June 1861	168	31 Dec. 1863
164	31 Dec. 1861	169	30 June 1864
165	30 June 1862	170	31 Dec. 1864
166	31 Dec. 1862	171	9 April 1865

Scales of Maps

The following are the representative fractions of those maps for which it was possible to calculate a scale. Note that these scales refer to the original edition of the atlas, not to later reprints which may be somewhat reduced.

2: 4(1:420,000) 6(1:90,000)
3: 1(1:36,500)
4: 1(1:85,000) 2(1:22,000)
5: 1(1:24,000) 2(1:12,500) 3(1:26,000) 5(1:320,000)
   7(1:19,500)
6: 1(1:49,000) 2(1:32,000) 3(1:23,500)
7: 1(1:125,000)
8: 1(1:170,000)
9: 1(1:10,600) 2(1:1,000,000) 3(1:115,000)
10: 1(1:170,000) 2(1:250,000) 4(1:620,000) 7(1:16,500)
    9(1:33,000)
11: 2(1:200,000) 5(1:19,000)
12: 1(1:11,500) 2(1:11,500) 3(1:90,000) 4(1:30,000)
    5(1:275,000) 6(1:160,000)
13: 1(1:24,000) 2(1:32,000) 3(1:38,500) 4(1:38,500)
    6(1:63,360)
14: 1(1:15,000) 2(1:14,000) 3(1:90,000)
15: 1(1:6,000) 2(1:120,000) 3(1:6,000) 4(1:39,000)
16: 1(1:300,000)
17: 1(1:145,000)
18: 1(1:90,000) 2(1:140,000)
19: 1(1:130,000) 2(1:27,000) 3(1:200,000)
20: 1(1:240,000) 2(1:25,000) 3(1:34,000) 4(1:34,000)
21: 2(1:25,000) 4(1:67,000) 5(1:63,360) 7(1:23,000)
    9(1:310,000) 11(1:33,500) 12(1:30,000)
    13(1:350,000)
22: 1(1:225,000) 2(1:32,000) 3(1:26,000) 4(1:27,000)
    5(1:715,000) 6(1:130,000) 7(1:185,000)
23: 2(1:750,000) 3(1:450,000) 4(1:318,000)
    5(1:300,000) 8(1:150,000) 10(1:150,000)
24: 1(1:20,000) 2(1:67,000) 3(1:1,000,000)
    5(1:400,000)
25: 2(1:12,700) 4(1:25,500) 5(1:32,000) 6(1:1,000,000)
26: 2(1:22,000) 3(1:105,000) 4(1:86,000)
27: 1(1:400,000) 2(1:45,000) 3(1:37,000)
28: 1(1:38,000) 2(1:55,000) 3(1:35,000) 6(1:22,500)
29: 1(1:62,000) 2(1:31,000)
30: 1(1:33,000) 2(1:418,000) 3(1:43,000) 4(1:43,000)
    5(1:1,128,000)
31: 1(1:39,000) 2(1:250,000) 4(1:80,000) 5(1:24,000)
32: 1(1:24,000) 2(1:7,200) 3(1:45,000) 4(1:5,600)
    5(1:205,000) 6(1:140,000)
33: 1(1:39,000) 2(1:2,500,000) 6(1:276,000)
34: 1(1:130,000) 2(1:150,000) 3(1:143,000)
    4(1:135,000) 5(1:150,000)
35: 1(1:135,000) 3(1:25,500) 5(1:125,000) 6(1:164,000)
36: 1(1:275,000) 2(1:29,500)
37: 1(1:26,500) 2(1:41,000) 3(1:26,000) 4(1:150,000)
    5(1:36,000) 6(1:34,000) 7(1:18,000)
38: 1(1:41,000) 2(1:18,000) 3(1:13,600)
39: 1(1:36,000) 2(1:127,000) 3(1:90,000) 4(1:72,000)
40: 1(1:39,000) 2(1:34,500) 3(1:535,000) 4(1:750,000)
    5(1:35,000)

41: 1(1:80,000)
42: 1(1:33,000) 5(1:48,000)
43: 1(1:59,000) 2(1:46,500) 3(1:51,000) 5(1:42,000)
    7(1:1,400,000) 8(1:3,200,000) 9(1:25,000)
44: 1(1:1,400) 3(1:120,000) 4(1:2,675)
45: 1(1:200,000) 2(1:400,000) 3(1:63,360) 6(1:110,000)
    7(1:22,500) 8(1:30,000)
46: 1(1:45,000) 2(1:45,000) 3(1:155,000)
47: 1(1:2,300,000) 2(1:37,000) 3(1:37,000) 4(1:59,000)
    7(1:100,000) 8(1:69,000)
48: 1(1:280,000) 2(1:17,300)
49: 1(1:47,000) 2(1:64,200) 5(1:38,000)
50: 1(1:80,000) 2(1:50,000) 3(1:25,000) 4(1:25,000)
    5(1:240,000) 6(1:500,000)
51: 1(1:400,000) 2(1:31,000) 4(1:35,000)
52: 1(1:300,000)
53: 1(1:420,000) 3(1:35,000) 4(1:372,000)
54: 1(1:2,750,000) 2(1:26,500) 3(1:14,500)
55: 1(1:44,000) 2(1:42,000) 3(1:26,000) 4(1:44,000)
    5(1:48,000) 6(1:94,000)
56: 1(1:25,000) 2(1:40,000) 3(1:60,000) 4(1:37,500)
    5(1:31,000) 6(1:26,000) 7(1:21,000) 8(1:70,000)
57: 1(1:500,000) 2(1:155,000) 3(1:500,000)
58: 1(1:155,000) 2(1:480,000) 3(1:57,000) 4(1:40,000)
    5(1:34,000) 6(1:32,000)
59: 1(1:32,500) 2(1:19,700) 3(1:134,000) 4(1:18,500)
    5(1:23,000) 6(1:26,500) 7(1:28,000) 8(1:28,000)
60: 1(1:130,000) 2(1:130,000)
61: 1(1:28,000) 3(1:21,500) 5(1:4,000) 6(1:33,000)
    7(1:25,000) 8(1:18,500) 9(1:672,000) 10(1:28,000)
    12(1:25,000) 13(1:26,500) 14(1:29,000)
    15(1:43,000)
62: 1(1:120,000) 2(1:20,500) 3(1:22,500) 4(1:92,000)
    7(1:36,500) 9(1:258,000) 10(1:155,000)
    12(1:375,000) 13(1:127,000) 14(1:235,000)
63: 1(1:6,200) 3(1:105,000) 4(1:225,000) 6(1:19,700)
    7(1:55,000) 8(1:80,000)
64: 1(1:18,000) 2(1:8,500) 3(1:12,300) 4(1:18,000)
65: 1(1:120,000) 2(1:108,000) 3(1:373,500)
    4(1:32,000) 6(1:16,500) 7(1:40,000) 8(1:6,300)
    9(1:43,000) 10(1:1,120,000)
66: 1(1:1,116,000) 2(1:163,000) 3(1:110,000)
    8(1:102,000) 9(1:102,000) 10(1:2,475) 11(1:85,000)
67: 1(1:20,500) 3(1:400,000) 4(1:6,100) 7(1:19,000)
    8(1:19,000) 9(1:68,000)
68: 1(1:13,000) 2(1:13,000) 3(1:41,000) 4(1:7,300)
    5(1:21,000) 6(1:36,000) 7(1:17,500)
69: 1(1:130,000) 2(1:130,000) 3(1:130,000)
    4(1:120,000) 5(1:900,000)
70: 1(1:750,000) 2(1:22,500) 3(1:50,000) 4(1:32,000)
71: 1(1:230,000) 2(1:230,000) 3(1:250,000)
    4(1:250,000) 5(1:280,000) 6(1:280,000)
    7(1:280,000) 8(1:250,000) 9(1:250,000)
    10(1:250,000) 14(1:23,500) 15(1:400,000)

72: 1(1:24,250) 2(1:53,000) 3(1:29,000) 4(1:10,750) 5(1:11,000) 7(1:25,000)
73: 1(1:45,000) 2(1:38,000) 3(1:30,000) 4(1:23,000) 6(1:37,000)
74: 1(1:800,000) 2(1:43,000) 3(1:26,000) 4(1:17,000)
75: 1(1:13,500) 2(1:7,000) 3(1:13,100)
76: 1(1:900,000) 2(1:4,000,000) 3(1:12,500) 4(1:73,000) 5(1:305,000)
77: 1(1:110,000) 2(1:110,000) 3(1:97,000) 4(1:50,000)
78: 1(1:220,000) 2(1:53,000) 3(1:183,000) 4(1:57,000)
79: 1(1:38,000) 2(1:42,000) 3(1:660,000) 4(1:20,500) 5(1:51,500) 7(1:24,000)
80: 1(1:350,000) 2(1:315,000) 3(1:335,000) 4(1:317,000) 5(1:317,000) 6(1:317,000) 7(1:380,000) 8(1:380,000) 9(1:380,000) 10(1:19,500) 11(1:32,000)
81: 1(1:160,000) 2(1:160,000) 3(1:160,000) 4(1:880,000) 6(1:500,000) 7(1:40,000)
82: 1(1:38,000) 2(1:51,500) 3(1:1,000,000) 4(1:55,000) 5(1:85,000) 6(1:31,000) 7(1:46,000) 8(1:31,500) 9(1:40,000) 10(1:41,000) 11(1:46,000) 12(1:90,000)
83: 1(1:40,000) 2(1:40,000) 3(1:46,000) 4(1:35,000) 5(1:31,000) 6(1:31,000) 7(1:40,000) 8(1:40,000) 9(1:31,000)
84: 1(1:32,000) 2(1:80,000) 3(1:80,000) 4(1:190,000) 5(1:63,360) 6(1:53,000) 7(1:40,000) 8(1:60,000) 9(1:1,000,000) 10(1:970,000) 11(1:48,000)
85: 1(1:1,170,000) 2(1:29,500) 3(1:350,000) 4(1:43,000) 5(1:85,000)
86: 1-7(1:507,000) 8-16(1:570,000)
87: 1(1:27,000) 2(1:125,000) 3(1:63,360) 4(1:128,000) 6(1:7,500)
88: 1(1:50,000) 2(1:500,000)
89: 1(1:63,360) 2(1:14,000)
90: 1(1:75,000) 2(1:131,200) 3(1:66,200) 6(1:77,000) 7(1:87,000) 8(1:28,500) 9(1:56,000)
91: 1(1:110,000) 2(1:80,000) 3(1:486,000) 4(1:1,000,000)
92: 1(1:120,000)
93: 1(1:250,000) 2(1:58,500)
94: 1(1:320,000) 2(1:430,000) 3(1:63,360) 4(1:160,000) 6(1:125,000) 7(1:125,000) 8(1:135,000) 9(1:135,000)
95: 1(1:23,000) 2(1:23,000) 3(1:625,000)
96: 1(1:50,000) 2(1:39,000) 3(1:52,500) 5(1:125,000) 6(1:51,000)
97: 1(1:402,000) 2(1:54,000) 3(1:33,000)
98: 1(1:2,200,000)
99: 1(1:27,000) 2(1:37,000)
100: 1(1:670,000) 2(1:160,000)
101: 1(1:230,000) 3(1:230,000) 4(1:245,000) 6(1:200,000) 7(1:24,250) 8(1:138,500) 10(1:222,000) 11(1:275,300) 12(1:186,000) 13(1:18,000) 14(1:18,600) 17(1:21,500) 21(1:730,000)
102: 1(1:13,000) 2(1:7,600) 3(1:38,500)
103: 1(1:21,000) 2(1:45,000)
105: 1(1:26,500) 2(1:38,000) 4(1:65,000) 5(1:300,000) 7(1:24,000) 8(1:225,000) 9(1:79,000)
110: 1(1:305,000)
111: 1(1:149,500) 4(1:9,875) 5(1:25,500) 6(1:15,000) 9(1:250,000) 10(1:13,000)
112: 1(1:18,000) 3(1:10,000)
114: 6(1:24,000)
115: 1(1:18,000) 2(1:13,500) 3(1:17,000) 4(1:18,000) 5(1:18,500) 6(1:28,000) 7(1:5,250) 8(1:17,500) 9(1:17,500)
116: 1(1:31,000) 2(1:320,000) 3(1:90,500) 4(1:636,000)
117: 1(1:2,100,000)
118: 1(1:2,250,000) 2(1:400,000) 3(1:65,000)
119: 1(1:1,900,000)
120: 1(1:2,650,000) 2(1:903,000)
131: 1(1:77,000) 2(1:42,000)
132: 1(1:120,000) 2(1:6,000) 3(1:6,800) 4(1:6,100) 8(1:68,000)
133: 1(1:32,000) 2(1:26,500) 3(1:145,000) 4(1:5,750)
134: 1(1:2,000,000)
135: 1(1:32,500) 3(1:80,000) 5(1:100,000)
135A: 1(1:3,168,000)
135B: 2(1:43,000) 3(1:25,000) 4(1:5,300)
135C: 1(1:749,000) 2(1:134,000) 4(1:63,360) 5(1:34,000)
136-161: 1:633,600
162-173: 1:7,000,000

For Reference

Not to be taken from this room

NEW HANOVER COUNTY PUBLIC LIBRARY

3 4200 00400 1141

For Reference

Not to be taken from this room

NORTH CAROLINA ROOM
NEW HANOVER COUNTY PUBLIC LIBRARY

NCR